Stories from the HISTORY OF ROME

Mrs. Emily Beesly
illustrated by Bartolomeo Pinelli

PURPLE HOUSE PRESS *PH* KENTUCKY

Published by
Purple House Press
PO Box 787
Cynthiana, Kentucky 41031

Classic Books for Kids and Young Adults
purplehousepress.com

Written in 1878 by Mrs. Emily Beesly
Illustrated by Bartolomeo Pinelli, 1817-19
Images courtesy of the Rijksmuseum, Amsterdam
Gift of J.J. de Man, Ede, 1929
Illustration on page 112 by Bartolomeo Pinelli, 1821
Copyright © 2024 by Purple House Press
Unabridged
All rights reserved

ISBN 9798888180990

Contents

	Preface	iv
1	The Building of Rome	1
2	The Horatii and the Curiatii	6
3	Brutus and his Sons	16
4	How Lars Porsenna Besieged Rome	21
5	Caius Marcius and His Mother	29
6	The Deeds of the Fabii	43
7	Cincinnatus	53
8	The Battle of Corbio	59
9	How the Romans Won Two Cities	65
10	The Taking of Rome	76
11	The Gulf in the Forum	91
12	The Story of Titus Manlius	94
13	The Death of Decius	105
14	The Caudine Forks	114
15	The Two Fabii	127
16	How Pyrrhus Fought Against Rome	133

PREFACE

THE WRITER of this little book was not satisfied that her children should hear nothing but fairy tales and the stories of nursery life, now so popular. But she could find nothing else fit to read to them. There are, indeed, plenty of story-books drawing their materials from history, and professing to be intended for children. But they are not suited to very young children. They abound in words and ideas which a child of four or six years old not only does not understand, but cannot be made to understand. The writer, however, believed that it was quite possible to put portions of Livy and Plutarch into language which should need little or no explanation even to children of that age. She accordingly made the experiment. One story after another was written and read to her little boys. Whenever she discovered that a word or idea was unintelligible to them, she took pains to simplify it. She found that they thoroughly enjoyed these old tales from Roman history, and liked to hear them repeated again and again. She has thought, therefore, that if published they might perhaps supply a want that may have been felt by other parents.

It was necessary that the stories should be such as would interest little children. But the writer has also selected them with a view to illustrate the two sentiments most characteristic of Roman manners—duty to parents and duty to country. She has, moreover, tried to indicate that the latter of these sentiments took precedence of the former. A healthy moral lesson is thus conveyed, while at the same time the most essential feature of the Roman civilization is impressed on the memory.

Probably no one will be found to raise the dull objection that many of these tales are not strictly true. Being typical of Roman manners, they are true in a more real sense than many a well attested but less, characteristic fact. They undoubtedly helped to create in Romans those virtues which they professed to record. To the young, aye, and to older persons, it is more important to have heard that Brutus beheaded his sons and that Mucius thrust his hand into the flame, than to be acquainted with the most approved theories as to the origin of the Plebs or the functions of the three Comitia. May it be long before these old legends are banished from Roman history in the name of a pedantic and unprofitable accuracy!

Mrs. Emily Beesly, 1878

Senatus Populusque Romanus
The Senate and People of Rome

The Building of Rome
Chapter One

THERE ONCE reigned in a town called Alba in Italy a king whose name was Numitor. He had a brother called Amulius, who was a proud and wicked man, and could not bear that his elder brother should be king over him. So Amulius plotted against his brother. He got together a number of men who were as bad and cruel as himself, and they attacked Numitor and drove him from his throne, and made Amulius king in his stead. They took the sons of Numitor, and his daughter Rhea Silvia, and killed them. Then Amulius seized the two little sons of Rhea Silvia, who were still only babies; he gave them to his soldiers, and told them to throw the poor little boys into the River Tiber.

"Then," thought he, "they will be drowned. There will be none of my brother's children left to trouble me, and I shall be king all my life."

The soldiers took the two babies in their cradle, lying side by side fast asleep, and carried them to the river.

Now, there had been a great deal of rain, and the Tiber had overflowed its banks, so that the men could not put the children in the deep part of the river, but only at the edge, where the water was shallow. However, they thought that they would have obeyed the orders of Amulius if they left the little boys there. So they put the cradle down in the water, and went away.

But the sun was shining, and the waters were sinking fast; soon the dry land began to show itself; the cradle stood still, and the waters left it on the bank and ran back into their bed.

There lived not far from the Tiber a shepherd whose name was Faustulus. He was walking by the side of the

Romulus and Remus suckled by the she-wolf

river, when he saw a cradle lying under a fig-tree, and beside the cradle stood a great she-wolf. Faustulus was very much astonished, and ran quickly to see what this might mean. When he got near, he saw that in the cradle were two beautiful little baby boys, and the wolf was feeding them with her milk, just as if they had been her own little ones. But when she saw Faustulus, she fled away into the woods; and he took the children and carried them home to his wife. So these two kind people loved the boys and brought them up like their own sons.

Romulus and Remus, so the boys were called, grew up strong and bold and active. They did not care to till the ground and herd the cattle, but loved to hunt in the woods and mountains. Sometimes, too, they would attack the robbers whom they met in that wild land, and take their plunder from them. So, it happened that many young men from the country round came to them and joined their expeditions, and of these Romulus and Remus were always the chiefs and leaders.

Faustulus had heard that two grandsons of the king had been thrown into the Tiber, and he guessed that these must be the boys he had found. When Numitor, their old grandfather, heard of these two young men, he too thought they must be his daughter's sons. Then Romulus and Remus took their friends and companions with them, and went to Alba. They attacked King Amulius and killed him. When Numitor heard of what had happened, he called the Alban nobles together, and told them of all the wrongs he had borne from his brother, and all the story of his grandsons. While he was still speaking, the two brothers marched with their followers into the midst of the assembly, and they hailed their grandfather as King of Alba, to the great joy of all the Alban people.

Now Romulus and Remus were not content to stay at Alba with their old grandfather; but they determined to build a new city for themselves. They made up their minds that this new city should be near the River Tiber, on the spot where they were found by Faustulus when they were little babies. So they took their companions with them, and went to that place. There was still growing the fig-tree under which their cradle had lain, and they resolved that they would build their walls there, and leave the fig-tree standing in the midst. For hundreds of years afterwards the fig-tree was to be seen standing in one of the chief streets of Rome.

The walls were soon begun, but while they were building, the two young men began to quarrel. Remus spoke scornfully to his brother and laughed at him, and jumped over the wall that Romulus had just begun to raise. Romulus was very angry, and in his rage he struck his brother and killed him.

Thus he became the only leader and king. He finished building the city, which he called Rome after his own name. He ruled it for many years, and after his death the Romans worshipped him as a god.

The triumph of Romulus

THE HORATTI AND THE CURIATII
Chapter Two

IN THE REIGN of King Tullus Hostilius there was a quarrel between the people of Rome and the people of Alba. The Romans and the Albans were generally very friendly to each other. They were of the same race; their way of living was the same, and they spoke the same language. Some of the Romans had married Alban women, and some of the Albans had married Roman women, so that each people had friends and relations in the other town.

But now there was a quarrel between them, and the Roman army with King Tullus at its head marched out to meet the Albans, who were commanded by their Dictator, Mettius Fufetius.

When the armies came near together, the Alban Dictator sent a messenger to King Tullus. The messenger came to the Roman army, and was led before the king, who was preparing himself for the battle.

Now, Tullus was a brave warrior; he was young and strong, and eager to win glory in war; but still he was wise, and he did not refuse to listen to the message of

Mettius. "O Tullus," said the messenger, "I am sent to you by the Dictator of the Albans. He bids me tell you, that it will be much for the good of Rome as well as for the good of Alba if you will come out in front of your army, and speak with him before the fight begins."

Tullus agreed to do as Mettius asked. The two armies took their places, and all was made ready for battle; and then Mettius and Tullus, followed by some of their nobles, advanced midway between the armies, and Mettius spoke these words,—

"Hear me, King Tullus, and you nobles of Rome. It seems to me that the only cause of our quarrel is that we know not whether Rome or Alba is the stronger, and which town shall be the master of the other. Can we not decide this in some other way than by the death of all the brave men who must be slain if we begin to fight?"

The thought pleased King Tullus, and after consulting together, they fixed upon a plan. It was agreed that three Romans should fight against three Albans, and that if the Romans conquered, Rome should govern Alba; but if the Albans were victorious, then Alba should govern Rome.

It happened that in the Roman army there were three brothers called Horatius, all strong men and brave soldiers. They were the sons of an old Roman named

Publius Horatius, who had taught them, as Roman fathers in those days taught their sons, that they ought to be ready to die for the good of their people and their dear city of Rome. That was the first duty of every Roman, and you shall hear how the Horatii kept their father's sayings.

The Roman army felt that they could choose no better champions than these three brothers. And the Horatii proudly and gladly agreed to fight, and each in his heart resolved to do his very best to save his country from being subject to Alba.

Now in the Alban army there were also three brothers, whose name was Curiatius. They too were

The Horatii proudly agree to fight for Rome

good soldiers, and their countrymen chose them to fight for Alba. These three brothers were friends of the Horatii, such dear friends that one of them had promised to marry the sister of Horatius. But they loved their town of Alba, and like the Romans they felt that they must lose their own lives, or take those of their friends, for the sake of their country.

When the Roman King and the Alban Dictator had promised solemnly that Rome and Alba should keep the agreement, the three brothers on each side took their weapons and marched out between the two armies. The soldiers of both towns sat down on each side, to watch the fight, with anxious hearts, knowing that the fate of their country depended on the courage and skill of those few men.

At first the battle seemed very equal, for the six were all good soldiers and full of bravery; their hearts were set on winning the victory, and they were not thinking of the wounds or death that they might suffer in the struggle. But soon it seemed that the Albans were getting the better, for two of the Romans were killed, but the Albans were all wounded. The Alban army shouted for joy; they thought their victory was won, as they saw the three Curiatii surround the one Horatius who was still alive and unhurt. But cries of anger broke from the

Romans when they saw their last champion turn and fly from his enemies.

"Shame on the coward!" they cried; "the name of Horatius is disgraced for ever. Better he had died gloriously doing his duty like his brothers."

But they soon saw that Horatius was no coward, and that his flight was only a way to separate the three Albans, who all together would have been more than a match for him. Horatius knew that all the Curiatii were wounded. As he fled they followed him, and soon the one who was least wounded came up to him. Horatius turned instantly to attack him. The combat was fierce,

Battle between the Horatii and the Curiatti

and lasted for some time; the Roman and Alban armies eagerly watched the two champions, and the two other Curiatii tried hard to reach their brother to help him. But they were wounded and could not move fast, and before they could come up they saw their brother fall. Still they came forward; the one who was least wounded hastened on, and Horatius, joyful with his victory, stepped out to meet him. The Alban, bleeding and out of breath with the haste he had made, had no chance with the conqueror; and the third brother, dragging himself on with difficulty, yet with no thought of yielding, saw him die, and knew that he was left alone.

Then Horatius sprang forward to meet him, crying out,—

"Two of these brothers have died by my hand. Now the third shall follow them, that Rome may rule over Alba!"

Having said this he stabbed Curiatius, and so died the last of the Alban brothers.

When the Romans saw that their enemies were slain they shouted for joy, and Mettius the Alban Dictator came to King Tullus, and asked him if he had any commands for him; for he remembered the agreement that had been made between them before the fight began. Tullus told him to take his army safely back to Alba, but he said that the Albans must keep themselves ready to help him in war, if he should want them.

So the armies departed to their homes, after having buried the five brothers who had fallen. The graves of the two Romans were together; those of the Albans were separate, in the places where they died. Hundreds of years afterwards their tombs were still to be seen.

Great was the joy in Rome when news came from the camp that Horatius was victorious; the people decked their houses with garlands and hung them with bright-coloured cloths, and came in crowds flocking to see the brave man who had saved Rome. The army marched in at the gate of the city, and in the front came Horatius, carrying in his hands the swords of the three Curiatii, and wearing on his shoulders the mantle that one of them had worn. And the people cried to the gods to bless their champion, and the women threw flowers and laurel boughs on his helmet and under his feet as he went along.

But there was one person in Rome whose heart was sad that day, and that was the sister of Horatius, when she heard that her brother had killed the man who was in a little while to have been her husband. In her grief and despair she ran out to meet Horatius, with her head uncovered and her hair loose on her shoulders; and

THE HORATII AND THE CURIATII 13

when she met him she saw that he was wearing the mantle that she herself had embroidered and given to Curiatius. Then, in a voice of sorrow, she called out the name of Curiatius, and told Horatius that he was a cruel brother to her, because he had killed the man she loved so well.

The words she said made Horatius very angry.

"What," cried he, "do you forget your two brothers who are dead, and your brother who is still alive, and your country, which I have this day saved!"

Then in his rage he drew his sword, and stabbed his sister to the heart, so that she died, saying,—

Horatius kills his sister, Camilla, as an enemy of Rome

"So may it be done to every maid who is a Roman, and weeps for the death of an enemy!"

The people of Rome were very much shocked at what Horatius had done, and they took him and led him before the king, who then spoke to the people, and said,—

"I will choose two judges to judge this man, and to say what shall be done to him."

And so he did. Then the judges said that Horatius must be slain. But he cried out, and said,—

"Let me be tried by the whole people, and let them say if I deserve to be punished."

So the king called the people to meet together to try Horatius for having killed his sister. And when the people were assembled Horatius came before them, and with him was his old father, Publius Horatius.

In Rome a father was able to do as he pleased with his son, even after the son had grown up to be a man—he could sell him as a slave, or put him to death, or punish him in any way he chose; but Publius Horatius did not wish to give his son a severe punishment, for he thought that his daughter deserved to die. The father and the son were of the same temper—they loved their country better than they loved their family.

The old man stood up before the people and spoke to them.

"My daughter," said he, "has been rightly punished, for she forgot her duty, and loved a stranger better than she loved Rome. Do not take away from me my last child, but remember that I have already lost two brave sons, who died in battle for their country."

Then he threw one arm round his son, and pointing with the other hand to the armour and weapons of the Curiatii, which had been hung up on a pillar in the open square where the people were met,—

"O Romans," he cried, "could you bear to see this young man die shamefully, whom you saw a little while ago marching as a victor through the streets of Rome? Would you chain these hands which have just won freedom and empire for the Roman people? Where would you kill him? Inside the walls where you see the spoils and weapons which he won from your enemies, or outside the city in sight of the graves where the Curiatii lie buried?"

The people were sorry to see his father's tears, and were surprised that Horatius himself showed no fear of death; they wondered at his courage, and remembered that he had saved them from being subjects of Alba, and they said,—

"We will pardon Horatius, because he has done such great things for the good town of Rome."

Brutus and his Sons
Chapter Three

THE LAST KING who reigned in Rome was called Tarquin the Proud. The Romans hated him because of his pride and cruelty; and at last his wickedness and the wickedness of his sons enraged the people so much, that they rose against him, and drove him and all his family away from Rome. The people resolved that they would never more have a king to govern them, but that they would choose two of the best and bravest nobles of Rome to be their rulers. These two chiefs were called consuls, and they were to govern the city for one year only, after which new consuls were to be chosen.

The two first consuls were Collatinus Tarquinius and Lucius Junius Brutus. Both of these men had been leaders of the people in driving out the king. Both were relations to Tarquin, and both had suffered great wrongs from him. Lucius feared that Tarquin would kill him, as he had killed others of the chief men of Rome, and for years he pretended to be so stupid and foolish that the people gave him the surname of Brutus, which means foolish.

But when the people of Rome at last rose up against the wicked Tarquin, Brutus put himself at their head, and soon showed by his wise and brave conduct that he had been only acting or pretending to be stupid, that he might live unharmed by the cruel king.

Tarquin for a long time tried hard to get back to Rome. Among the young Roman nobles were several who had been friends of the young princes, and who would have been glad to bring the Tarquins back, for they

Brutus and Collatinus swear to banish the Tarquin from Rome forever

cared more for their own amusements than that the people should be free. Two of these young nobles were Titus and Tiberius, the sons of Brutus.

These young men met together one night to talk over their plans, and they wrote letters to Tarquin telling him they were ready to help him, and sent messengers to him with the letters. But it happened that a slave named Vindicius was in the room where they met. He did not mean to watch what they were doing, but he saw them come hastily into the room with anxious faces, and feeling afraid, he hid himself behind a large chest, and so heard all that was said.

When they had gone away Vindicius came out of his hiding place, and was at first greatly puzzled what to do. He was afraid to go to the Consul Brutus, and to tell him that his two sons were plotting to bring King Tarquin back. At last he determined that he would go to Valerius, a noble Roman who from his great love for the people was afterwards called Poplicola, which means the people's friend.

So Vindicius went to Valerius, and told him all his story. Valerius was very much astonished, and ordered that Vindicius should be kept safely in his house, while he himself went, with as many armed friends and slaves as he could get together in a hurry, to the house of one of the plotters. They broke open the doors, and found the letters to King Tarquin in the room of the messengers, who had not yet started on their journey.

The consuls sat to judge the people in the Forum, or market place, with their lictors beside them. The lictors were the consuls' guards, and were armed with a bundle of sticks or rods in which an axe was tied up; and they punished any one who was condemned by the consuls, either by beating him or by cutting off his head.

The young men were brought before the consuls. When they were accused of plotting to bring back the king, and the letters found by Valerius were read aloud, and the story of the slave Vindicius had been heard, they did not dare to say that they were not guilty.

The people were sorry for Brutus when they saw his sons led before him to be judged, and some said,—

"Would it not be punishment enough if the young men were banished for all their lives from Rome?"

Collatinus, the second consul, shed tears, and Valerius did not speak a word. But Brutus looked sternly on his sons.

"Titus and Tiberius," he said, "why do you not answer to the accusation these men bring against you?"

Three times he asked them this question, but still they did not dare to answer a word, for they knew they were guilty and deserved to be punished. Then Brutus turned to the lictors.

"You," said he, "must do all the rest that has to be done."

So the lictors seized the young men, tied their hands behind them, beat them with their rods, and afterwards cut off their heads. Then Brutus left his seat and went home to his own house.

Brutus sentences his sons to death

How Lars Porsenna Besieged Rome
Chapter Four

When King Tarquin was driven out of Rome he went to Clusium in Etruria, where reigned a great and powerful king called Lars Porsenna. Tarquin hoped that by the help of Porsenna and his Etruscan allies he might be able to conquer the people of Rome and so make himself king again. So he came before Porsenna and begged for his help.

"Do not," he said, "allow these Romans to banish us from their city. Remember that kings should be always ready to help each other; for if the peoples of Italy see that the Romans can drive out their king without being punished for it, they too will try to get rid of their kings, for all men love freedom."

Porsenna listened to all that Tarquin said. He was sorry for the old man, who had been obliged to fly from his kingdom, and he promised to help him. He collected a great army, and accompanied by Tarquin and his sons, marched towards Rome, hoping to be able to take it at once. This he could not do, because the brave Horatius Cocles defended the bridge over the Tiber, and so gave the Romans time to cut it down.

Horatius defends the Ponte Sublicio

When Porsenna found that he could not take Rome at once as he had hoped, he determined to besiege the city, that is, to encamp his army round it, and watch it well so that no one could either go in or out, and so that no food could be brought in. He also got ships and boats to guard the River Tiber, so that no one should get into the town that way.

Porsenna sent his soldiers all round the city, and they plundered the country close to the walls, so that the people were obliged to drive their flocks of sheep and herds of cattle inside Rome.

One day the Consul Valerius ordered that a large flock of sheep should be driven out of the town, and the Etruscan soldiers, hearing of this, came eagerly to drive them off to their camp. But Valerius laid his plans well, for he sent the brave Herminius and Spurius Lartius who had helped Horatius to defend the bridge, each with a party of Romans, to hide themselves some little way outside the walls. The Etruscans came up and were beginning to drive off the sheep, when Valerius had the gates of Rome opened and marched out to attack them with a strong party of soldiers. As soon as Herminius heard the trumpets, which were the signal that Valerius had begun the fight, he led his men out of their hiding place and charged the Etruscans on the other side. The Etruscans would now gladly have fled away, but as they tried to go towards their camp Spurius Lartius and his troop met them, and so, surrounded and overpowered, they were all killed.

But still the siege went on; and as there was not much food left in the city, Porsenna began to hope that the Romans would soon be obliged to yield.

There lived in Rome a young man called Caius Mucius, who thought it was shameful that the Roman people should be besieged now that they were free.

"For," said he, "such a thing never happened to the city before, even when the kings governed it. And now, are we to be kept prisoners within our walls by these Etruscans, whom we have so often beaten in fight?"

So he resolved that he would try to force his way into

Porsenna's camp, and do some great deed there. He went to the Senate to ask for leave to go on his expedition.

"Fathers," said he, "I have a great wish to cross the Tiber, and get into the enemy's camp if I can; not as a robber, but because I wish to do some great deed if the gods will allow me."

The Senators granted what he asked; and Mucius set off, carrying his sword with him hidden under his clothes.

When he arrived in the camp of the Etruscans he found a great crowd near the tent of King Porsenna, for the soldiers were going to receive their pay. Mucius saw a man in splendid garments sitting and giving orders; and thinking this must be the king, he rushed up to him and stabbed him. But this man was not the king, but one of his nobles. Then the Etruscan soldiers seized Mucius and dragged him before Porsenna.

The king asked the young man who he was, and why he had killed the Etruscan?

"I am a Roman," answered Mucius boldly. "My name is Caius Mucius. I wished to kill you, King Porsenna, because you are the enemy of Rome; and I am not afraid to die since I have not done what I meant to do. A Roman ought to be able to do and to bear great things. But I warn you, I am not alone; for I have many followers who are resolved to kill you. You must be ready at all times to fight for your life; and see that you have armed men always watching to guard you. For we, the young men of Rome, declare war against you. Look here, and see how little Romans fear pain."

As he spoke he stretched out his right hand and thrust it into the fire that was burning near the king.

Porsenna was greatly astonished at the bravery of Mucius; he sprang up from his throne, and bade his soldiers set the young man free.

"You have been more cruel to yourself, Mucius, than to me," he said. "I set you free. Go home untouched and unharmed by any Etruscan."

Caius Mucius casts his right hand into the fire

"Since you value courage so much," said Mucius, "I will tell you what your threats should never have made me say. Three hundred young Romans have vowed to kill you. The first turn was mine; but the rest will come, one after another, until one shall succeed in killing you."

When Porsenna heard this he began to think, though he was a brave man, that he certainly would never get back to Clusium, as some one of these fierce Romans would be sure to kill him.

But Mucius went safely back to Rome, and after this time he was always called Scævola, which means the left-handed, because his right hand was burnt.

And Porsenna sent ambassadors, or messengers, to Rome to offer to make peace with the Romans. He tried to make them promise to let the Tarquins come back to Rome; but they would not consent to that. At last Porsenna gave up all thoughts of making Tarquin King of Rome again, and he promised to lead his army away, if the Romans would give him hostages, that is, would give him some of their own people as prisoners; so that he might be quite sure they would keep the peace for fear of what he might do to these prisoners. So the Romans gave him a number of young boys and girls. Porsenna marched away, but pitched his camp again on the banks of the Tiber, not far from Rome.

One day, when the Roman maidens, who were Porsenna's hostages, were walking beside the Tiber, one of them whose name was Clœlia thought how easy it would be to get across the river away from their enemies, as Horatius Cocles had done. She spoke to the other girls and bade them do as she did. She then plunged into the water, and swam across. She was soon on the other side, followed by her companions, and it was not long before they were all once more with their friends in Rome.

Porsenna was very angry when he heard that the Roman maidens had escaped. He sent at once to the

Clœlia courageously crosses the Tiber

consuls, bidding them give him back his hostages, or he would not keep the peace. The Romans sent the girls back to him, for they wished honourably to keep the promises they had made. Porsenna was so much pleased with their honesty, and with the courage of Clœlia, that he set her free, and allowed her to choose any of her companions whom she wished to take back with her to Rome.

So peace was made again between the Romans and the Etruscans; and the Romans so honoured the brave Clœlia that they had a statue made of her, and placed it in one of the chief streets of Rome, called the Via Sacra, which means the Holy Street.

Caius Marcius and his Mother
Chapter Five

THERE WAS a noble lady in Rome named Volumnia, whose husband had died, leaving her with one little son, who was called Caius Marcius. Volumnia was a brave and noble woman, and she spent all her time in bringing up her son, and in making him what she thought a Roman ought to be—brave and honourable, and able to bear toil and hardship. And Caius loved and honoured her, and made her happy by obeying her and trying to please her in every way. But he had a proud and haughty temper, and was often fierce and even cruel to those whom he did not love. In person he was strong and active, and from his childhood he loved to learn the use of weapons. As he grew older he practised himself constantly in wrestling, racing, and all kinds of manly games, and thus he became so strong and skillful and swift of foot that none of the young men of Rome could compare with him.

When Caius was still very young he went out to war for the first time, when Aulus Postumius led the Roman army to fight against the proud King Tarquin, and won the great victory at the Lake Regillus. Caius Marcius behaved with great bravery in this battle, and after the fight was over the general gave him a crown of oak leaves—the reward usually given to a soldier who had saved the life of a Roman. How glad must Marcius have felt when he came back to Rome and met his mother's eyes, and knew that she was proud of her dear son!

From this time Marcius was always eager to win fame in war; and he was never satisfied with what he had done, but always tried to do more and more glorious deeds. He thought himself most happy when he could return to Rome after having fought bravely, and bring his spoils and his triumphal garlands to his mother, that he might see her joy in his glory.

Now a war broke out between the Romans and the Volscians, and the Consul Cominius led an army against a Volscian town called Corioli, and besieged it. Then, leaving part of the army with Titus Lartius, a very brave old officer, Cominius went towards Antium, another Volscian town, to meet the Volscian army. While he was gone the men of Corioli came out of their town, and attacked a party of Romans who were under the command of Marcius. He and his soldiers beat back the attack of the Volscians, and drove them into the city. Then Marcius cried out,

"The gates are open for the conquerors as well as for the conquered."

And, so saying, he with very few following him rushed into Corioli in pursuit of the Volscians. In the town he fought with the greatest bravery and the Volscians could not drive him out till Lartius and his army came to help him, and so the town was taken.

The Roman soldiers at once began to plunder Corioli; but Marcius told them it was shameful for them to be collecting spoil and plundering, when the Consul Cominius and his troops were perhaps at that very moment fighting the Volscians. He put himself at the head of those who were willing to go with him, and got to the place where Cominius was just as the battle was going to begin. Marcius begged the consul to let him fight in the place where the danger was the greatest; and the consul admiring his courage granted what he asked.

When the battle began, Marcius charged the Volscians with such fury that he broke through their ranks, and he was in great danger, and badly wounded, but the consul sent his own guards to help him, and the Volscians were put to flight. The soldiers then begged Marcius to go to his tent that his wounds might be dressed and he might rest himself; but he only said, "It is not for conquerors to be tired," and he joined them in pursuing the enemy.

Next day the consul made a speech to the army, and he praised the gallant deeds of Marcius.

"Of all the plunder that we have gained," he said, "we will give the tenth part to Marcius, who has so well deserved it; and I myself wish to give him a beautiful horse, to show him how much I admire his valour."

Marcius came forward before the army to answer the consul.

"I must refuse the reward you offer me," he said; "I cannot take a bribe to pay my sword. I will take my one share like the other soldiers. But your horse I will accept —and besides I will ask a boon. I have a friend among the Volscian prisoners, and I would ask for his freedom."

All the army praised Marcius for his generosity, and the consul said,

"We will give to Marcius a reward that he cannot refuse; and that is, that from this day he shall be called Coriolanus, after the town of Corioli, which he won for Rome."

Soon after this there was a great famine in Rome. During the wars and troubles of the last year the land had not been tilled, and the seed corn had not been sown; so now very little corn was to be had, and the people could hardly get bread to eat. But a great deal of corn was brought from Sicily, and the Senate met to talk over the rate at which the people should be allowed to buy it—that is, how much money they must pay for it.

Now, Caius Marcius—or Coriolanus, as he must now be called—was, as I told you, a very proud man. He thought because he was rich and of a noble family, that he was better than the poor plebeians, as the common people of Rome were called, forgetting that a poor man may be as good and as brave as a rich one; and that a working man may love his country just as well, and be as ready to die to serve it as the greatest noble. He wished that the nobles—the patricians they were called in Rome—should have the power to govern the country as they pleased, and that the common people should have no voice in the matter. He was also very angry because some time before the Senate had allowed the people to choose some men called tribunes, who were to defend any poor man who was in trouble, and in all sorts of ways to do all they could to help the plebeians against the nobles.

When the Senate met to fix about selling the Sicilian corn, Coriolanus stood up and made a speech to them.

"If the people," said he, "want this corn to be sold to them as cheaply as it used to be, let them give back to the Senate all the power it used to possess. Shall we, who could not endure to have the Tarquins ruling over us, submit to these low-born tribunes? Let us make the people give them up to us, and never have another tribune in Rome. If the people want corn, let them steal it, as they did three years ago, if they will not do as the Senate bids them."

When the people heard of what Coriolanus had said, their anger was very great.

"Coriolanus," they cried, "would make us do his will by starving us, the people of Rome, as if we were enemies. He will take from us this foreign corn, which is our only chance of getting bread for our children, unless we give up our tribunes to him. He will either make us slaves, or force us to die of hunger."

They ran to attack Coriolanus, and he might have been killed, but the tribunes came between, and ordered him to be tried for what he had said. At first he treated the threats of the tribunes with scorn; but the rage of the people was so great that the Senate were afraid, and thought it best to punish Coriolanus rather than that there should be war in the city. So he was tried, and was condemned to be banished, or sent away from Rome for all his life. The people were much delighted at this sentence, and the nobles were in the greatest distress; so that it was easy to see by men's faces to what party

Coriolanus is tried by the tribunes

they belonged—he who looked glad and cheerful was a plebeian, and he who looked downcast and sad was a patrician.

Coriolanus himself was the only one who did not show any grief. He was too proud to do so. He went home to his own house and bade farewell to his wife and mother, who were in the greatest sorrow. He told them they must bear this trouble patiently, and then he left them, and went out of the city. He resolved that he would go to the country of the Volscians, for his anger was so great against the Romans that he hoped to be able to revenge himself on them by the help of their old enemies.

So he came to Antium, where lived Tullus Aufidius, the greatest warrior among the Volscians. Coriolanus went into the house of Tullus without anyone noticing him, and sat down by the fire, covering his face with his cloak. The people of the house were much surprised when they saw him, but so grand and noble were his look and manner that they dared not speak to him or ask him any questions. At last they went to Tullus himself, who was at supper, to tell him about this stranger.

Tullus rose directly and went to the unknown guest, and asked him who he was. Coriolanus stood up, and uncovering his face,

Coriolanus is exiled from Rome, leaving his family behind

"I am Caius Marcius," he said, "the man who has done so much to harm the Volscians. For all the hard toil and danger that I have gone through I have no reward but the name of Coriolanus. The ungrateful and envious people of Rome have driven me away from their city. I come to ask if you will let me help you to fight against the Romans; for now instead of loving them I hate them, and will do my best to punish them, and to fight for you."

Tullus was greatly pleased to hear what Coriolanus said.

"Take courage, Marcius," answered he. "We accept your offer of help, and you shall find that the Volscians will be more grateful to you than the Romans have been."

And from that day Coriolanus lived in the house of Tullus, and they were friends.

Not long after this there was a quarrel between the Volscians and the Romans, and the Volscians chose Coriolanus and Tullus for their generals. It was agreed that Coriolanus should lead an army of Volscians to attack the Romans at once, and that Tullus should remain behind, to collect fresh troops, and to see that the Volscian towns were properly defended.

The Volscians were greatly pleased with the courage and warlike skill of their new general; and they praised him so often and so much, that Tullus began to think that all his own deeds would be forgotten, and he grew jealous of Coriolanus, and wished that he had never helped him to make friends with the Volscians.

News was brought to Rome that the banished Coriolanus, at the head of a large Volscian army, was marching to attack them, and soon they heard of his taking one town after another that lay between Rome and the country of the Volscians. At last he arrived at a place only five miles from Rome, and then all the people were in the greatest terror. The women ran up and down the streets in their fear, the old men were seen weeping and praying before the altars of the gods, and the whole city was filled with confusion and alarm.

The people and Senate agreed to send messengers to Coriolanus to beg him to put an end to the war, and to ask him to come home and be a Roman once more. So they chose for messengers men who were all friends or relations of Coriolanus, supposing that he would treat with respect and kindness those whom he had loved before he was banished. But when the messengers came to the Volscian camp, they were led before Coriolanus, who was seated in state, with his chief officers about him. He received them with a very severe manner, and as if they had been all strangers to him. He told them that the Romans must give back to the Volscians all the lands they had taken from them in former wars.

"If you do not do this," said he, "you shall have no peace."

So the messengers went back to Rome, sad at heart, to tell the people of these hard terms. The Romans in great fear sent the messengers back again to Coriolanus, but he refused to let them come into his camp. After this the priests in their robes went to try if they could persuade him to show mercy, but they could not alter his resolve. He told them that the Romans must either give up their lands, as he had said, or fight.

Now when the Romans had almost lost the hope of being able to defend themselves against their terrible enemy, some of the Roman ladies went to Volumnia, the mother of Coriolanus, to ask her and his wife, Virgilia, to go to him, and to beg him to spare the city. When the ladies had spoken, Volumnia said,

"All the Romans are unhappy, but we are more unhappy than all. For we see my son, Virgilia's husband, fighting against his own country. I know not if he have any love for us left, as he has none for his country, which used to be dearer to him than mother, wife, or children. But we will go to him if you wish it. If he will not listen to us, we can at least die at his feet begging him to have mercy on Rome."

So Volumnia and Virgilia took the two little sons of Coriolanus with them, and went with the other women to the Volscian camp.

When they got there the soldiers allowed them to pass through it, till they came to where Coriolanus was sitting among his chief officers. The general, who had resisted the prayers of his dearest friends, and of the priests who begged him in the name of the gods to spare Rome, was not inclined to pay any attention to a band of sorrowing women; but one of his attendants cried out suddenly,

"If my eyes do not deceive me, general, yonder stand your mother and your wife and children!"

Coriolanus was greatly surprised; he sprang from his seat, and ran to embrace his mother. But when he came near her she bade him stop.

"Before you embrace me," she said, "let me know if I am come to my son or to an enemy—if I am your mother or a prisoner in your camp. Has my life lasted so many years only that I should see you first banished, and now the enemy of Rome? Could you plunder the country in which you were born, and which has fed you for so many years? Did not your anger grow less when you came into these parts? Did not you think, when you came in sight of Rome, 'Within those walls is my home; there are my mother, wife, and children?' If you had not been born Rome would not have been attacked. If I had never had a son I might have died a free woman in a free country. Now what I suffer is shameful to you and most sad to me; yet, however miserable you make me, it cannot be for long, for if you go on to conquer Rome, you must pass over the dead body of your mother."

Then she and his wife and children threw themselves on their knees at his feet, and begged him to have mercy on Rome. Coriolanus was shocked to see his mother kneeling before him.

"O mother," he said as he raised her up, "what have you done? You have gained a great victory for Rome, but it will be ruinous to me. I go, conquered by you alone."

Coriolanus is conquered by his mother

So he sent the ladies back to Rome, and next morning he led the Volscian army away to Antium.

Some of the Volscians were very angry with Coriolanus because he had not gone on and conquered Rome, and among these was Tullus Aufidius. Tullus was also jealous of Coriolanus, because his great courage and skill in war had made the Volscians think more of him than they did of Tullus.

Tullus therefore resolved to kill Coriolanus, and collected a number of his friends who agreed to help him. They called on Coriolanus to give an account of what he had done before Rome to the people of Antium; and when he stood up to speak, they cried out that a traitor ought not to be heard, rushed on him, and stabbed him. So he died; but the Volscians gave him an honourable funeral, and raised a monument to his memory.

The Deeds of the Fabii
Chapter Six

THERE WAS in Rome a great family of nobles called the Fabii. There were a great many of them, brothers, cousins, and other relations, and they were brave men and good soldiers, but proud to the people. So the commons hated them, and were very angry because the nobles year after year got one or another Fabius made consul. The people thought that one of these men, Quintus Fabius, had not divided fairly the plunder that had been taken in war from the Volscians, and for this they hated the Fabii more than ever; and they hated the nobles too, for so often making Fabii their consuls.

These quarrels grew so violent that one year when Kæso Fabius was consul, and led the army against the Veientians, the soldiers would not fight. Fabius had more trouble with his own soldiers than with the enemy. He was a good general and drew up his troops in order of battle; but when he commanded them to charge, the foot-soldiers would not move; they hated the consul so much that they felt they would rather bear the disgrace of being beaten than help to win a victory for him. The horse-soldiers, however, who were rich men and did not belong to the common people, and did not hate the Fabii, charged the Veientians, and defeated them without the help of the foot.

The nobles still would not do as the people wished, and the next year they chose Marcus Fabius, Kæso's brother, for one consul, and Cnæus Manlius for the other.

The Etruscans were very glad when they knew how the Romans were quarrelling among themselves; for now they thought Rome might be conquered, as its own people would not fight to defend it. The Roman consuls were more afraid of their own soldiers than of the enemy, and they thought the best thing they could do was to shut themselves up in their camp, hoping that the soldiers would after a time change their minds and wish to fight. The Etruscans used to ride up to the gates of the camp, and challenge the Romans to come out and fight them. Sometimes they would tell them that they only pretended to quarrel because they were cowards and dared not fight. Sometimes they would say that the consuls would not let them fight, because they knew the Romans would be sure to be beaten.

The consuls did not care or take much notice of the taunts of the enemy; but the soldiers could not bear them so well. Their hearts were filled with shame and anger; and at last they crowded to the consuls' tent begging them to give the signal for battle. The consuls were glad enough to see the change in their men, but they would not yet yield. They wished to fight, but they thought if the soldiers were kept still a little longer in the camp that they would grow more and more eager for battle. So they spoke to the soldiers, and told them that the time for attacking the enemy was not yet come, but that they would stay in the camp.

The soldiers went away from the consuls, thinking that they were not to be allowed to fight, and wishing to do so more than ever. The enemy too, hearing that the consuls would not fight, came up to the gates of the camp and mocked and insulted the Romans, saying that they were not to be trusted with their arms, lest they should use them against their own generals. The Romans could bear it no longer, and ran in crowds to the consuls, demanding with shouts and cries to be led to battle.

Marcus Fabius, having talked with Manlius, the other consul, commanded the soldiers to be silent, and then said—

"I know, Manlius, that these men can win the battle

if they choose, but I know not whether they really mean to win it. So I have resolved not to give the signal for battle unless they swear that they will come back conquerors. For they will not dare to disappoint the gods."

One of the centurions (or officers), called Flavoleius, came forward, and said, "Fabius, I swear that I will come back a conqueror from the fight. If I do not, may the gods punish me."

All the rest of the soldiers made the same promise, and when this was done Fabius gave the signal, and the army marched out of the camp, full of hope and shouting to the Etruscans—

"Now let us see if you dare call us cowards again."

The Etruscans were eager for battle, thinking that the Romans would not really fight. But they soon found that they were mistaken, for they had hardly time to get into order, before the Romans rushed upon them, sword in hand. The people and the nobles all fought well that day, but the Fabii fought best of all, and gave a noble example for their countrymen to follow. One of them, Quintus Fabius, was in front of the Roman army, and he attacked the enemy so fiercely that he was separated from his own men, and surrounded by his foes. An Etruscan stabbed him with his spear, and he sunk down and died. The fall of this brave man made the Romans stop and then begin to go back; but Marcus Fabius, the consul, stepped across his brother's body and cried out to the soldiers—

"Was this what you promised me, fellow-soldiers? Did you swear that you would come back beaten to the camp? I made no promise; but now I swear I will either win the battle, or else die at your side, dear Quintus Fabius."

Then Kæso Fabius, who had been consul the year before, stepped up to the side of Marcus.

"Think you, brother," said he, "that you can make these men fight by talking to them? Instead of telling them, let us show them what to do, as is fitting for brave men, and men of the Fabian race."

When he had said these words the two Fabii at once attacked the enemy, and they were followed by the whole army.

Meantime, Manlius the other consul had been so badly wounded in another part of the battle, that he was obliged to go out of the fight, that his wounds might be bound up. This made his soldiers lose heart; they thought he was killed and were beginning to give way, when the Consul Fabius rode up to them with some of his horse soldiers, and called to them that he had conquered the other wing of the Etruscans, and that Manlius was not dead but only wounded. This cheered them, and soon after, to their great joy, Manlius came back to the battle. Meantime the Etruscans, who were many more in numbers than the Romans, sent a body of troops to attack the Roman camp, which they did so fiercely that they broke into it though the Roman guards defended it bravely.

News was brought to Manlius of what had happened, and he immediately came to the camp and set a guard of soldiers at each gate to prevent the enemy getting out. They tried hard to break through, and in the fight Manlius was killed. The Etruscans managed to get through the gate, but as they marched away they were met by the Consul Fabius and his conquering army, and many of them were killed and the rest put to flight. Thus the Romans had gained a splendid victory, though it was saddened by the deaths of Quintus Fabius, and of the Consul Manlius.

The Senate were very glad to hear of the battle being won, and they sent word to Marcus Fabius that he should enter the city in triumph with his army. But Fabius answered,

"My family are all in tears and grief for the death of my brother Quintus, and Rome is mourning for her consul. So I will not wear the laurel wreath, nor come home in triumph."

This refusal of Fabius was thought by the people more glorious than any triumph could have been. Splendid funerals were made for the two dead chiefs, and Fabius made speeches at the graves and gave them the praise that they deserved for so bravely dying for Rome.

Fabius did not forget that he had determined when he was first made consul to make the people friends again with the nobles. One of the things he did to bring this about was to plan that the nobles should give money to feed and clothe the poor soldiers who had been badly wounded in the war. And none of these soldiers were better taken care of than those who were the charge of the Fabian family. By these and other brave and kind deeds the Fabii made the people love them and forget their old dislike.

Soon afterwards new wars began with several peoples round Rome; but the most troublesome enemies of all were the Veientians. Then the Fabian family went to the Senate, and Kæso, who was consul again that year, spoke for all the rest.

"Fathers," he said, "it is well known to you that to fight the Veientians, a small number of soldiers always ready would be more useful than a larger number who would only be sometimes watching them. Do you attend to the other wars, but give the war against Veii to the care of the Fabian family. We promise you that we will not disgrace the name of Rome, and we will pay the cost of the war ourselves."

The Senate thanked the brave Fabii, and the consul with his family returned to their homes. Next day all the Fabii armed themselves, and met together in front of the consul's house. The consul saw all his family drawn up in order of battle, and he went out clad in his armour, and joined them. He gave the signal to start, and they all, three hundred and six in number, all nobles, all of one family, and each man fit to be a general, marched through the city to the gate nearest to Veii. They were followed by crowds of people praising them, admiring them, and bidding them go on bravely and fight successfully. So the Fabii left Rome, and marched on till they came to the River Cremera, where they built themselves a strong fort or castle, and there they watched the Veientians. They were so strong and brave that they kept their fort safe, and defended the country which borders on Etruria, and troubled the Etruscans greatly for some time.

The Etruscans got together an army and attacked

the castle, but the Romans sallied out and drove off the enemy, and afterwards defeated them in several other battles.

The Etruscans began to think that they could never conquer these fierce Fabii in open fight, so they made a plan to attack them unexpectedly. A number of Etruscan soldiers hid themselves not far from the castle. Then some others drove a flock of sheep out on to the plain further away from it. When the Fabii saw the sheep they went out to catch them, and in doing so they passed the place where the Etruscans were hidden. Then they scattered themselves about the plain in pursuit of the

The Fabii showed incredible valor at the Battle of Cremera

sheep, and suddenly met some Etruscan troops who had been sent to attack them. At the same time the Etruscans who had been hidden rushed upon them from behind, so that they were quite surrounded. The Fabii fought nobly, as you may fancy from what you have heard of their deeds; but they were few and the Etruscans were many, and they were killed, every one of them, except one young boy.

Cincinnatus
Chapter Seven

There was a people near Rome named the Æqui, who were at one time friends and allies of the Romans. But they broke the treaty of peace they had made with Rome, and marched an army towards Tusculum. They burnt the villages, and plundered the people, and then pitched their camp on Mount Algidus. The Romans sent ambassadors to the camp of the Æqui, to complain of their having broken the treaty, and to ask that all the plunder should be given back to the people to whom it belonged.

The general of the Æqui only laughed at the Roman ambassadors, and bade them tell the message of the Senate to a great oak tree which grew near the camp, and not to him. The ambassadors were very angry at this, and called upon the gods to punish the Æqui, who had so broken their promises of friendship.

When the Senate heard of the way in which their messengers had been treated, they collected an army, and sent it against the Æqui, under the command of one of the consuls, Minucius. Unfortunately Minucius was a timid man, and though he marched towards Algidus, and pitched his camp not far from that of the Æqui, he was afraid to fight a battle with them. The Æqui soon found out that the Roman general was afraid of them, and they grew bold, and attacked the Roman camp. Although they could not take it by storm, they dug ditches, and built mounds all round it, so that the Roman army was closely shut up, and could not get out. But before he was quite shut up, Minucius sent five soldiers out of his camp. These men managed to get through the enemy's guards, and made all the haste they could to Rome.

They went at once to the Senate, and told them that the consul and his army were besieged in their camp by the Æqui. Great was the sorrow in Rome when this bad news was heard. The Senate resolved to choose a dictator, and no man seemed to them so fit for their chief as Lucius Quintius Cincinnatus.

A dictator of Rome was like a king in most ways. He could do what he pleased, and all men were bound to obey him—but this only lasted for six months. After that time he was no longer dictator, and he could be punished if he had done any wrong in his time of power.

Messengers were sent at once to tell Cincinnatus what was fixed. He did not live in Rome, but in a little cottage outside the walls where he had a small piece of land; for though he was of noble family he was a very poor man.

The messengers found him hard at work, ploughing his little field. When they had greeted him, they bade him "put on his gown and hear what message the Senate sent him."

Cincinnatus was greatly surprised, and asked if all were well at Rome. Then he called to his wife Racilia to fetch him his gown out of the cottage, and having washed himself and put it on, he stood before the messengers. They told him that he was chosen to be dictator, and wished him joy.

"You must come at once to Rome," they said. "You are much wanted there, for the Consul Minucius and his

Cincinnatus was busy ploughing his field when chosen Dictator by the Senate

troops are besieged in their camp by the Æqui, and you must lead an army to set them free."

So Cincinnatus went to Rome. His relations and friends and most of the senators came to the gates to meet him, and led him into the town. Next day he came into the Forum or market place before it was light. He chose for his Master of the Knights, Lucius Tarquitius, who was said to be the bravest of all the young men in Rome. Then he commanded that the shops should be shut, and that no work should be done in the town; but that all men who were of fit age to fight should come together before sunset in a field close to the walls called the Campus Martius, or Field of Mars. Each man was to bring with him his arms, food for five days, and twelve wooden stakes. The men who were too old or not strong enough to fight, were to collect the food for the soldiers.

All was done as the dictator ordered, and when the soldiers were met together, he came to them and spoke to them in these words—

"Soldiers, we must make all the haste we can, that we may attack the enemy this very night. For the consul and his army have been besieged for three days, and we know not what may happen. Make haste, standard-bearer. March on, soldiers!"

The troops were eager to obey, and shouted as their general had done,—

"Make haste, standard-bearer. March on, soldiers!"

So they departed from Rome, and in the middle of the night they got to Mount Algidus, where the consul was still surrounded by the army of the Æqui.

Then Cincinnatus rode all round the enemy's camp to see, as well as he could in the night-time, how it was placed. Next he drew all his army in a long train quite round the camp, and commanded that when he gave a signal each man should shout as loud as he could, and then set to work to make a ditch in front of himself, and set up his twelve stakes as a paling to defend it. When all was ready the dictator gave the signal, and the Romans shouted so loud that the noise they made was heard not only in the enemy's camp, but by the Consul Minucius and his soldiers. Glad enough were the imprisoned army to hear the shouts of their countrymen and to find that help was so near. Minucius called his men together—

"Let us lose no time," he cried, "these shouts not only tell us that our friends have come to help us; they show that the Romans have already begun the battle. Stand to your arms, then, and follow me."

By this time the Æqui were doing their best to stop the soldiers of Cincinnatus from fencing them in; but while they were fighting the dictator's men on one side, they were attacked on the other by Minucius and his followers, who now rushed out of their camp, eager to set themselves free. So the Æqui were between two Roman armies. They fought well, and the battle went on all night, but when day came they were forced to yield and to beg for peace from Cincinnatus.

The camp of the Æqui was full of provisions and spoil, and the Romans took possession of it when the battle was over. But Cincinnatus gave all the plunder to the soldiers of his own army, for he was still angry with the consul and his troops.

"You soldiers," he said to them, "were very nearly made prisoners yourselves, and the spoils of the enemy are not for you. And you, Minucius, shall only command your army under my orders, till you have learned to be as brave as a consul ought to be."

So Minucius had to give up being consul, but stayed with the army as the dictator had commanded.

Although Cincinnatus was a severe general, he was so brave a man and so good a soldier that the army loved and admired him, and to show him their gratitude for his having saved them they presented him with a golden crown.

When he came back to Rome he was met with great joy by the people and entered the city in triumph. He then gave up his power, after having been dictator for only sixteen days.

The Battle of Corbio
Chapter Eight

Some years after the victory of Cincinnatus when Titus Quintius Capitolinus was consul for the fourth time, the Volscians and the Æqui again attacked Rome. They thought they could do so safely, because there were great quarrels in the city, between the nobles and the common people. They first attacked the Latins, who were now friends with the Romans, and then, finding that no army was sent to meet them, they marched on, plundering the country as they went, till they came up to the walls of Rome. Then having shown the Romans how little they feared them, and having collected a great deal of plunder, they marched away to Corbio.

Then the Consul Quintius called the people together, and spoke to them in these words—

"I come before you today, Romans, with the greatest shame that could be. You know, and our children's children will hear, that the Volscians and Æqui came in arms before the walls of Rome, and that no sword was drawn to resist them, in the year when Titus Quintius was consul. Had I known that such shame would have come upon me, I would rather have died or have been banished, than have been made consul. Which did our enemies think the most lazy and cowardly? Us consuls, or you Romans? If the fault is ours, let us be no longer consuls, or if that is not enough, punish us in what way you like. But if the fault is yours, O Romans, I would have you repent of your wrong doing, and I pray that neither gods nor men may punish you for it.

"Your enemies did not trust in your sloth, nor in their own courage, for you have beaten them so often in battle, that by this time they know both themselves and you. But the quarrels between the nobles and the commons are the ruin of Rome. What would you have? You wished for tribunes, and we granted them to you. We punished by death or banishment the noblest men of the city, because you were displeased with them. What will be the end of these quarrels? When shall we have peace within our walls? It is only against us nobles that you take up arms, not against the enemies of your country.

"But let me ask you to go out of the gates of the town, or, if you dare not do that, to look from the city walls into the fields. See how they are laid waste by fire and sword, the cattle driven away, and the houses smoking. The country is desolate, the city is besieged, and the glory of the war is with our enemies. What have you at home to make up for such losses as these? The tribunes will give you plenty of talk and words; but which of you ever took home to his wife and children, anything but quarrels and hatreds from these struggles in the city?

"But when you were soldiers under me, not under the tribunes—when you were in the camp, not in the Forum—when the enemy in the battle-field, not the Roman nobles in the Senate, heard and feared your shouts—then did you not return to your homes in triumph, loaded with riches, and crowned with glory? Stay here in the city if you please; but if you do not go to fight your enemies, they will come before long, to fight you here; they will scale the walls, mount the Capitol, nay, pursue you into your own homes.

"I know I might say many things that would please you better than this. And truly I would gladly please you, Romans; but yet I would much rather save you, whatever you may think of me hereafter. Oh, if you will but give up these quarrels, and do as your fathers would have done,

I will bear any punishment you please, if I do not in a few days drive these plunderers of our country out of their camp, and carry the war from our walls to their cities."

Never were the people more delighted with any speech than with this one of the consul, and they were eager for war. The army was ordered to meet next morning in the Field of Mars; the standards were brought out from the temple where they were kept in time of peace, and given to the soldiers; and the army with the two consuls at its head marched away from Rome. The next evening they pitched their camp near to that of the enemy near Corbio.

Now though there were two consuls, one of them, whose name was Agrippa Furius, thought that it would be much better that the army should be governed by one man; so he told the other consul, Quintius, that he would obey him in everything, and would do whatever Quintius thought best. Quintius was much pleased, and he praised Agrippa for caring more that the war should be well managed than that he himself should manage it.

When the Roman army was drawn up in line of battle, Quintius made Agrippa the leader of the left wing, that is, of the soldiers who fought on the left side of the army, and he himself led the right wing. The middle part of the army, the centre as it was called, was commanded by

Spurius Postumius. The battle began, and the centre and right wing of the Roman army fought bravely, and though the Volscians and Æqui resisted stoutly, yet the Romans began to get the better of them. Meantime the Roman cavalry, or horse soldiers, attacked the enemy's cavalry and defeated them and killed a great many. When they had done so they charged the rest of the Volscian army, by which they greatly helped their countrymen, and the enemy who were already beginning to give way were put in disorder, and yielded to Quintius.

But the left wing of the Roman army was in great trouble, for they could not conquer the part of the enemy's army which was opposed to them. Then the Consul Agrippa, who was a very strong man, seized the standards from the soldiers who carried them, and going up in front of the enemy, he flung the standards with all his force into the middle of them. The Romans would have felt it a terrible disgrace if they had lost their standards, and rushed forward so eagerly to win them back that they broke the ranks of the Æqui, and so the battle was won.

Just at this moment there came a messenger from Quintius to tell them that he was victorious, and just going to enter the enemy's camp; but that he waited to know if Agrippa had conquered too. If so, Agrippa was to come to Quintius at once, so that the whole army might join in winning the spoils of the enemy. Agrippa did as he was commanded, and after taking the camp, where they found great quantities of rich spoil as well as the plunder which had been taken from their own country, Quintius and he led their army back to Rome.

How the Romans Won Two Cities
Chapter Nine

THERE WAS a town called Veii, which was on the border of Tuscany, some miles from Rome. The people of Veii, who were called Veientians, had often fought against the Romans; their town was as large and rich as Rome, and they boasted that their courage and skill in war were as great as those of the Romans. The quarrel between the two towns was so fierce, that it could plainly be seen that whichever people was conquered, would be destroyed by the other—so that there must either be no Romans, or else no Veientians left.

There were many battles fought, and on the whole the Romans got the best of the fighting. But the Veientians were many and brave; they built strong and high walls round their city, got together plenty of food and arms, and so waited without fear for the coming of their enemies.

The Romans heard how strongly Veii was defended; they knew how difficult it would be to take the town, and how many of their brave soldiers would be killed if they tried to do so. So they determined to blockade the city, that is, to encamp their army round the town, and watch it well, so that none of the Veientians could get out, and so that no one could bring them food or help. They hoped that when all the food was eaten, and the Veientians were tired of being shut up inside their walls, they would yield, and give up their town.

The Roman army marched to Veii, and while the summer lasted it was pleasant enough for the soldiers to live in their tents in the warm sunny air. But when the winter came, and the weather grew cold and stormy, the Roman leaders made their men build huts and little houses where they might all be sheltered.

Now, before this time, the Romans were used to make war only in the summer, and they were very angry at being kept away from their homes and wives and children for so long. They said that never, even in the old times when they were governed by the kings, had they been obliged to make war in the winter.

The people of Rome wished to order the army to come home; but Appius Claudius, one of the senators, made a speech to them and persuaded them not to do so.

"If you call your army back from Rome now," said he, "the Veientians will immediately come out of their city, and will attack us and plunder our cornfields and vineyards, and burn our cottages and our orchards; and then our work will all have to be done over again next year. For we must conquer the Veientians, or else they will destroy Rome."

In this way he persuaded the people to let the army stay on at Veii. But the siege went on year after year, and still the Veientians would not yield up the town, and still the Romans would not go to their homes, but watched and waited.

In the seventh year after the siege was begun a strange thing happened. There was a lake among the hills, some miles from Rome, called the Alban Lake. Most lakes have rivers running through them; but the Alban Lake had no stream either flowing into it at one end, or out it at the other. The water in the lake began in this year to rise higher, nobody knew why; and at last it rose so high that it overflowed, and the water ran down the hills across the country towards the sea. This curious thing was very much talked of in all the country round, and in the Roman camp, so that at last it was heard of by the besieged Veientians,—for the soldiers of the two armies would sometimes talk together, as often happens in long sieges.

A Roman soldier was one day talking to an old Veientian, who seemed to be very much pleased when he heard the strange story of the Alban Lake.

"For," said he, "we have an old saying or prophecy in our town, that the Romans will never take Veii if the water of the Alban Lake gets down to the sea."

The Roman was very much surprised to hear this; and he pretended he wanted to ask some other questions of the old Veientian, who was said by his townsmen to be a prophet who could tell beforehand what was going to happen. So it was agreed that they should meet one another between the town and the camp without their weapons. When the time came, they met as had been fixed; but then the strong young Roman threw his arms round the old man, and in spite of all his struggles carried him off to the camp and took him before the Roman general, who sent him to Rome. There he was taken before the Senate, the assembly of nobles who governed Rome, who asked him what was the meaning of his strange words.

"It is written in some of our old books at Veii," answered the man, "that if the Romans make a new channel for the waters of the Alban Lake when they overflow, they shall conquer Veii; but they are doing nothing."

The Senate then determined to send messengers to the temple of Apollo at Delphi, to ask the god what they must do. The messengers, when they returned, brought word that the water must not be allowed to flow away into the sea, but that the Romans must dig ditches and canals for it to run in, till it had all run away in watering the land. This was done, but still the siege of Veii went on.

In the tenth year of the siege, the Senate determined to change the generals, and they made Marcus Furius Camillus dictator. Camillus was well known to the Romans as being a brave and successful soldier, and the army were very glad to hear that he was to be their new leader. But before he joined the army at Veii, he got together a large body of fresh troops, and led them out to meet the people of Falerii, another town near Rome, who had attacked the Roman lands, hoping to do so safely while the Romans were busy fighting the Veientians. Camillus defeated the Falerians in a great battle, and drove them out of their camp, after which he led his army to Veii.

Soon after he got there, he ordered his soldiers to make a mine into the town. A mine is a passage underground, which the soldiers of a besieging army dig so deep that it goes quite under the walls, and comes up inside the town. Camillus made his soldiers work by turns, so that day and night there were always some of them digging at the mine, and there were fresh men to take their places as soon as they got tired, so that none of them need do too much. In this way the work was carried on quickly; and the Veientians knew nothing about it, and had no idea that the Romans were digging a passage under their walls.

When the mine was ready, Camillus, with part of his army, made an attack on the outside of the city, and the Veientians ran to defend their walls. Meantime the king and the priests were offering sacrifices to the gods in the temple of Juno.

Now it happened that the underground passage had been dug so far, that the end of it was just under the pavement of the temple of Juno, and the Romans in the passage could hear all that was going on in the temple, and they heard the priest say—

"The gods promise victory to whoever shall offer this animal to them."

Upon hearing this the Roman soldiers broke through the pavement, rushed up into the temple, and offered the sacrifice to the goddess, while the Veientians, astonished and frightened by their shouts and the clashing of their armour, fled away. Some of the Romans pursued them, and others ran to open the gates to Camillus and the rest of the army; soon the city was filled with the Romans, and there was fighting in every part of it. Camillus told his officers to forbid the soldiers to hurt the women and children; but he let them plunder the town.

Then Camillus resolved that he would take the statue of Juno, the protector of Veii, to Rome. He chose out a number of young men from the army, and bade them wash themselves and dress in white garments, and then he went with them to the temple, and sacrificed to the goddess.

"O Juno," said he, "we pray thee to accept our service, and to go with us and live among the gods of Rome."

It is said that the statue gently answered him, that she was willing and ready to go. So they carried her to Rome, and Camillus built a stately temple for her on Mount Aventine.

Not long after the taking of Veii, the Romans gave Camillus the command of an army, which he was to lead against his old enemies the Falerians. He soon entered their country, and so much did they fear him, remembering how he had before defeated them, that they shut themselves up in their town of Falerii, which was built among rocky hills, and defended with strong walls. But when they saw the Romans marching over their lands, burning their villages and wasting their fields, they could bear it no longer. They came out of the town and pitched their camp among the rough rocks not far from the gates. Camillus was glad to be able to fight them, and one night he marched his army to their camp, so that at break of day the Falerians saw their enemies close upon them. The Romans attacked them fiercely, and the Falerians fled out of their camp and ran as fast as they could to the shelter of their city; but many were killed and wounded before they could reach the gates.

Camillus resolved to besiege the town; but it was well defended and strong, and the Falerians had collected plenty of corn and food and arms, so that the siege might have lasted as long as the siege of Veii, if a strange thing had not happened.

The Falerians felt so sure that the Romans could not break through their strong walls, that everything went on in the town just as if there had been no army encamped before it. The people went about their business or amusement, and the children went to school as usual. There was one schoolmaster in Falerii who taught the sons of most of the nobles of the town, and he used in time of peace to take the boys for walks and games outside the walls. After the siege began he still took the boys as usual just outside the gates of the town, and the Roman soldiers never took any notice of this; so the schoolmaster made a wicked plan. Every day he led the boys a little further and a little further from the town, keeping them amused with talk or play, so that they should not see what he meant to do. At last one day he took them further than ever, and right among the Roman soldiers. He bade the soldiers take him to Camillus, and he and the children were led into the general's tent.

"See here, general," he said. "See these children. In giving them to you I am giving Falerii to you, for these are the sons of the greatest and noblest men of town, who will do whatever you please in order to save their sons out of your hands."

Camillus listened to the schoolmaster till he had done speaking, and then he said:

"Thou art come, thou base fellow, with thy hateful present to a people and a general who are very different

Children of the Falerii

from thyself. We have never been allies of the Falerians, but we do not forget that we are men as well as they are; and that it is right to be just as well as brave. We do not draw our swords against children, but against soldiers. Thou hast tried to conquer Falerii by such a wicked deed as was never seen before; I will conquer by the help of the good swords and brave hearts of my Romans. Here, lictors, strip off this villain's clothes, bind his hands behind his back; give your rods to the boys, and let them flog him back to the gates of Falerii."

In the meantime the people of Falerii had found out what had happened. The city was filled with cries of grief, and the fathers and mothers of the boys ran to the walls or gates not knowing what to do, and fearing that they had lost their dear children for ever. While they were in this state of grief, what was their surprise and joy to see their boys coming over from the Roman camp driving their wicked master before them. The Falerians were so much moved by the generous conduct of Camillus, that they resolved to give up their town and to make peace. They sent messengers to Camillus, who bade them go on to the Senate at Rome, to whom they gave this message.

"We men of Falerii give ourselves up to you, O Senators, because we see that the Romans love justice better than victory. We think that we shall be better governed by you than by our own laws; nor shall you ever repent of your generosity, nor we of being under your government."

Both friends and enemies thanked Camillus for what he had done, peace was made, and the army came back to Rome.

These great victories made Camillus very proud, and many men in Rome began to envy him, and to think that he was growing too great. And after many quarrels they persuaded the Senate to banish Camillus from Rome.

The Taking of Rome
Chapter Ten

In the northern part of Italy there lived at this time a people called the Gauls. They were of the same race as the Scotch Highlanders, who are still sometimes called Gaels, and were a fierce and savage people who loved fighting. They are described to us as tall strong men with fair hair, who wore dresses of many colours, like the Scotch plaids, and were armed with shields and long broad-swords. It was many years before the time of which I am now telling you that the Gauls had first crossed the Alps, and settled in Northern Italy; but they now began to march further south, and attacked Clusium.

The people of Clusium sent to Rome to beg for help. The Senate refused to send an army to their aid, but chose three young nobles of the family of Fabius, as ambassadors to go to the Gauls, to try and make peace.

When the three Fabii arrived in the Gaulish camp they were led before the king, and spoke to him thus:

"The Roman Senate, O king, would have you put an end to the war against the Clusians who have never injured you. If it should be needful, know that the Romans will fight with you to defend their friends and allies; but they will gladly be at peace with you if you will stop fighting."

"We will make peace with the Clusians," answered the Gaulish king, "if they will give up to us a part of their lands. If not, we will fight them in your presence, Romans; and then you may go home and tell your fellow-countrymen how much braver the Gauls are than any other people."

"But," said the ambassador, "what right have you to come and take the lands of Clusium? What have you to do in Etruria?"

"That I will soon show you with this good sword," cried the Gaul fiercely. "A brave man has a right to everything."

So the ambassadors went back to Clusium, and all was got ready for fighting.

Now it has always been a rule among nations that an ambassador ought to take no part in war. He must not fight; and if he were to be harmed by any one of the people to whom he is sent, it would be a great wrong. But the Roman ambassadors, when they saw their Clusian friends march out against the Gauls, could not resist the pleasure of going with them. The battle began, and Quintus Fabius attacked the Gaulish general and ran him through with his spear. The Gauls soon found out that it was the Roman ambassador who had killed their general, and their rage against the Romans was so great, that they left off fighting the Clusians, and marched away to their camp to plan what should be done. Some of them wished to march straight to Rome; but the elder men determined first to send messengers to the Senate, to ask that the Fabii should be given up to them.

The Romans, however, instead of punishing the Fabii, praised them, and chose them to be chief officers in the army for the next year. When the Gauls heard of this their anger was very great, for they were a passionate and savage people, and they at once set out for Rome. The people in the towns and villages through which they passed were very much frightened at the wild and strange warriors; but they, when they saw the people trying to run away to save themselves, cried out in a loud voice that they would do them no harm, and that they were going to punish the Romans.

News soon came to Rome of the terrible enemy that was so near; and the Fabii and the other generals led out the army to meet them. The generals were careless and did not make great preparations, as they ought to have done, against their new foes. The soldiers too, instead of being eager for battle as they usually were, were very much afraid of these fierce strangers, whose arms and looks and ways of fighting were quite different from anything ever seen in Southern Italy before. And if they were afraid when they set out, they grew much more terrified when the two armies came near together, and they could hear the Gauls shouting out their war-songs and clashing their arms, as their wild and savage fashion was.

They met on the banks of the river Allia, eleven miles from Rome. Brennus, the king of the Gauls, led his army to the attack, and the battle did not last long, for neither officers nor soldiers in the Roman army behaved like Romans. They thought of nothing but of saving themselves, and turned and fled without striking a single blow. Many went to Veii, others tried to swim across the Tiber, and many were drowned there, being tired and weighed down by their heavy armour; many were slain by the enemy as they tried to escape; others got safely to Rome, and fled into the Capitol in such haste, that they did not even shut the city gates after them.

The Gauls were quite astonished by their easy victory, and for a while stood still as if they hardly knew what had happened. But at last, seeing that the Romans had all fled, they marched on and reached the city about sunset. When they found that the gates were open, and saw that no one came to resist them, they thought that the army must be concealed in the city ready to attack them if they went in. So, as the evening was coming on, they encamped outside the walls for the night.

In the meantime, the terror in Rome was such as had never been known there before. The Romans supposed that all their army had been killed except the small number who had escaped to Rome; for they did not know that a much larger number had fled to Veii. The whole city was filled with wailing and lamenting. As they had no hope of defending the city with so few soldiers, it was resolved that the young and strong men, with their wives and children, and the strongest of the senators, should go to the Capitol, which was a steep rocky hill defended with strong walls and towers.

Arms and food were got together, and taken to the Capitol. They thought if they could defend the temples of the gods, which were on this hill, and keep alive the strongest of the people and some of the senate, that the loss of the old people and of the rest of the city would have to be borne. And that the people who were left in the city might bear their fate more patiently, the aged nobles, many of whom were senators, and had been consuls, declared themselves ready to die with them; so that they might not be a burden to the small number of men who were able to fight.

Many of the people fled out of the city; some went to neighbouring towns, others wandered about in the fields. Some of the priests and priestesses (or vestal virgins as they were called) carried away the statues of the gods and other sacred things, and fled with them to a town not far off.

When all had been made ready for the defence of the Capitol, the old men went back into their houses. Those who had been consuls, or had held any other high office, clad themselves in their splendid embroidered robes, and seated themselves in their ivory chairs, and thus they waited for the coming of the enemy.

The Gauls spent the night outside the town, as I told you, but when morning came they marched in. They were much surprised to find no one in the streets, or public places; so after setting a small number of men to watch the Capitol, lest the garrison there should attack them unexpectedly, they began to go into the houses to look for plunder, and finding the doors of the great houses where the nobles lived unfastened, they first went in to them. There, to their great astonishment, they found the grand old nobles sitting in their chairs of state so still and quiet that the Gauls did not know if they were real men or statues of the gods. Then a Gaul stretched out his hand and touched the long white beard of Papirius, one of these old nobles, to see if he were alive. Papirius, angry at the insult, struck the rude soldier on the head with his ivory staff. At this the Gaul quickly drew his sword, and killed the old Roman. Then the slaughter began. The Gauls killed the old men, and plundered their houses, and then rushed into the other houses, plundering and setting them on fire, and killing the people who had not fled.

When the Romans in the Capitol saw their dear city

Papirius hits a rude Gaul with his ivory staff

full of enemies, plundering and burning and killing, and heard their shouts, the cries of the Romans, and the noise of the falling houses, they were full of misery and sorrow. They were so few that they could do nothing to help their friends; but their courage still did not fail them, and they resolved to defend the little hill which was all they had left to the very last.

After some days, when the Gauls had finished burning and plundering the city, they began to wish to take the Capitol too. First they made an attack upon it, and tried to climb up the sides of the hill. The Romans let them come half-way up, and then suddenly set upon them, threw them down the steep rocks, and killed a great many. So, finding that they could not take the Capitol by force, they resolved to lay siege to it. They left a small number of their warriors to guard it, so that no one should go in or come out, while others of their troops plundered the country round, or attacked the towns that were near.

I told you in the last story that the brave Camillus had been banished from Rome; he had gone to live in a town called Ardea. When he heard of all the misfortunes of his country, he was more unhappy than his own troubles had made him; and he wondered what had become of those brave soldiers who had fought with him at Veii and

Falerii. News was brought to Ardea that the Gauls were coming, and the terrified Ardeans asked Camillus what they should do. When he heard these things, he went to the Ardean Assembly, and spoke in these words to the people:

"My old friends of Ardea," he said, "I hope none of you think that I forget all the kindness you have shown me since I came to your city. And now in this danger it is fitting that every one should do what he can for the common good. How can I show you how grateful I am to you, better than at such a time? And how can I be of use to you except in war? For in my own country I had some fame as a soldier. Now, then, Ardeans, you have a chance of repaying the Romans for all their kindness to you, and also of winning for your city a glorious name in war. The people that are coming against you are men who are very big, but not so strong as they look. They are tired with the siege of Rome, and they wander about the country, filling themselves with meat and wine, which they get by thieving. When night comes on they lay themselves down without any camp or sentinels, in the fields or by the river sides, like so many wild beasts; and since their victory they are even more careless than they were before. Now, then, if you dare defend your town, stand to your arms when evening comes on, and follow me; and if I do not give you the chance to kill them like wild beasts when they are asleep, banish me from Ardea, as I was banished from Rome!"

Everybody before this believed that there never was such a man for war as Camillus, and the Ardeans now followed his advice. As soon as it grew dark, they met him at the city gates. He led them out, and they had not gone far before they came to the place where the army of the Gauls lay sleeping. There were no guards nor sentinels, so the Ardeans rushed upon them, and killed great numbers of them, unarmed and asleep. Of the rest of the army, some were killed by the people of other towns near Ardea, and some fled away to their fellow-countrymen at Rome.

In the meantime the part of the Roman army which had gone to Veii was getting larger; for not only more Romans came to join them, who had fled from Rome when the Gauls took it, but many soldiers came in from the towns of Latium to help them. When they heard of the victory that Camillus had won over the Gauls, they determined to ask him to come and lead them. They did not like to do this without asking the leave of the senators at Rome; yet it was a difficult thing to get to them, as they were on the Capitol surrounded by the army of the Gauls. A young man called Pontius Cominius offered to do his best to take the message. He easily got to the Tiber, and then swam down the river till he came to Rome. The side of the Capitol nearest the river was a very steep craggy rock, and the Gauls did not watch it as carefully as the other sides, thinking that no one could climb it. But Pontius crept out of the river, managed to scramble up the rock, and so got into the Capitol. He was taken to the senators, and gave them his message from the army at Veii. They were very glad to hear the good news he brought, and sent word to the soldiers that the Senate recalled Camillus from banishment and made him dictator. The young man then went back the same way that he had come, and got safely to Veii.

Now, though Pontius got safely away, he had not been able to help leaving on the rocks the marks of where he had scrambled down, and the Gauls, when they saw these footprints, found out that some one had been up the cliffs which they thought could not be climbed.

"If the Romans can get up, why should not the Gauls do the same?" said one of the boldest of them. And the next night, when it was dark, he climbed up. When he came down, it was resolved that a party should go up and attack the Romans while they were asleep. So they began to climb, helping one another and pulling one another up as best they could, all without speaking a word.

Now the Romans, trusting in the steepness of the rocks, kept careless guard; they were all asleep, and so quietly did the Gauls come up that no one heard them; even the dogs slept on. But in one of the temples near the walls there were some geese which were sacred to Juno the goddess of that temple. These geese were disturbed by some sound that the Gauls made, and began to cackle and clap their wings. They made such a noise that they awoke Marcus Manlius, a brave Roman, who had been consul three years before. Springing up, and seizing his weapons, Manlius ran out to see what was the matter. When he came near the temple, what was his surprise to

The Gauls attack the Capitol

see the tall figure of a Gaul standing on the wall at the top of the rock. Manlius shouted to the other Romans to follow him, and rushing at the Gaul he gave him such a blow with his shield, that he knocked him right off the wall and down the rocks outside. The fall of this man knocked down some of those who were standing below him, and frightened the others so that they dropped their weapons. By this time the other Romans had joined Manlius, and they threw their spears and large stones down upon the Gauls, putting them into such fear that they fell down the rock, and many of them were killed.

Next morning the soldiers were called together before the generals, who praised Manlius for his bravery; but they ordered that the sentinel who ought to have been watching the part of the wall where the Gauls climbed up, should be thrown down the rock.

After this both the Roman and Gaulish guards kept better watch. But now both parties began to be troubled by want of food, and many of the Gauls fell ill and died. They were used to live in a much cooler country, and the heat of Rome made them ill. The Romans, too, were quite tired of being shut up in the Capitol. Their food was nearly finished, the soldiers grew so weak that they could hardly bear the weight of their arms, and they began to think that the dictator Camillus would never come to drive away the Gauls. So both parties were very glad to make a truce, that is, to agree that they would not fight each other for several days. The Romans said they would make any conditions the Gauls liked, and the Gauls said they would go away if the Romans would give them a thousand pounds weight of gold. The Romans agreed to this, and Sulpicius, one of the generals, was sent to Brennus the king of the Gauls to pay him. The gold had to be weighed, for it was not in coins, such as we have, but in lumps. The Gauls tried to use weights which were not fair, so as to get more gold than they ought to have had. Sulpicius saw this, and told them it was unfair and

Camillus liberates Rome from the Gauls

shameful. Then King Brennus threw his sword into the scale, exclaiming, "Woe to the conquered!"

The weighing was not yet done, when, to the joy of the Romans, the dictator Camillus and his soldiers arrived. When he saw what they were doing he was very angry.

"Begone," he said to the Gauls, "and do you, Romans, take away that gold."

The Romans at first said they could not obey him, and told him what they had promised before he came.

"The promise cannot be kept," he answered, "no Roman had any right to make such a promise without the leave of the dictator."

Then turning to Brennus, he bade him get his men ready for battle.

The Gauls seized their arms, and attacked the Romans with more rage than skill. They were driven back and forced to fly, and at last had to march out of the city. The Romans followed them, and another battle was fought about eight miles from Rome in which the Gauls were all killed, their camp was taken, and not one man was left to carry the news back to their own country.

The Gulf in the Forum
Chapter Eleven

SOME YEARS after the taking of Rome by the Gauls, the people of Rome were greatly troubled by a strange thing that happened in the city.

The ground in the middle of the Forum, or market place, split and sunk down to a great depth, leaving a large hole or gulf so deep that no man could tell where the bottom of it might be. The Romans tried to fill it up, and threw in cartloads of earth and stones; but it was of no use. However much they threw in, the gulf still seemed to be as deep as ever; do what they would, they could not find the bottom.

So wonderful a thing, the people thought, must be caused by the anger of the gods. They enquired of the prophets, and begged them to pray to the gods, and to say what the Roman people must do to win pardon.

At last the prophets brought their answer, which was as follows:—

"If the Roman people would have their republic last forever, let them throw into the gulf the best and most precious thing that there is in Rome."

Then all the people began to consult and talk together, that they might find out what was the most precious thing in Rome. Some said gold, and others jewels, and others corn. Some said one thing and some another.

But a brave young man called Marcus Curtius came forward, and said,

"There is nothing in Rome so precious as the brave heart and good weapons of a Roman."

Then, when all were silent, he looked at the temples of the gods that stood on the Capitol and could be seen

The self-sacrifice of Marcus Curtius

from the Forum, and stretching his hands out first towards heaven and then towards the deep gulf at his feet, he vowed to sacrifice himself for Rome.

He then put on his armour, and mounting his good horse rode to the gulf and leaped in, while crowds of men and women flung fruit and flowers in after him. The earth closed over him; and for hundreds of years afterwards the place where the gulf had been was called the Curtian Pool.

The Story of Titus Manlius
Chapter Twelve

The Romans were taught from their childhood that they ought to love their country more than any other thing. They were also taught that it was their duty to obey their father, and that he might do anything he pleased with them. Even if a Roman father were cruel or unkind, his son would have been thought very bad if he had not been obedient and dutiful to him. To show you how real and strong this feeling was, I will tell you the story of Titus Manlius.

There lived in Rome a man of noble family called Lucius Manlius, who, because of his proud and stern temper was surnamed "The Imperious." He was made dictator, and raised troops in Rome to fight against a neighbouring people called the Hernicans.

Lucius Manlius had one son, whose name was Titus. This young man was not clever, and stammered when he spoke; his father treated him unkindly, for he would not let Titus live in Rome, but sent him away into a country village, where he lived with the rough peasants, and had no chance of being able to learn and improve himself.

The Romans did not like the proud Manlius, and when his time of being dictator was over one of the tribunes of the people, called Marcus Pomponius, brought a complaint against him. Pomponius said that Manlius had been very cruel and severe in his way of raising the troops.

"He has," said the tribune, "taken a great deal of money from the people, and has imprisoned them and had them beaten. Besides all this, he has kept his own son, who has done no wrong, away from the city and his home, putting him to hard and rough work; and treating the young man like a slave instead of like the son of the greatest man in Rome. And why has Manlius done all this? Because the poor young man could not speak well, but stammered in his talk. Ought he not rather, if he had been a kind father, to have been more tender to his son, instead of punishing him for what was not a fault but a misfortune?"

When Titus Manlius heard that his father had been accused of cruelty to him, he was very angry, for he was an obedient son, and he thought that he ought to do and bear whatever his father wished. He was so unhappy that his father should be brought into trouble on his account, that he set off at once for Rome. He arrived there very early in the morning, and went straight to the house of the tribune Pomponius.

When Titus asked to see the tribune, the servants told him that he was still in bed; but they went and told their master that the son of Manlius had come, and wanted to speak to him. The tribune hoped that Titus had some complaint to make against his father, and sent for him to come in.

When they had saluted each other, Titus spoke.

"I must see you alone, Pomponius," he said, "for I have a secret which none must hear but you."

The servants left them, and as soon as they were alone Titus drew a dagger from his belt, and standing over the tribune—

Titus Manlius forces Marcus Pomponius to withdraw his charges

"Swear to me," he cried, "that you will never call the people together to judge my father, or I will stab you at once!"

The tribune was dreadfully frightened when he saw the dagger glitter before his eyes. He was alone and unarmed; the young man was strong and active, and really meant to do as he had said. So Pomponius was obliged to swear that he would go no further in his accusation against the elder Manlius.

The people were very sorry that they could not punish this stern and cruel man, for the tribune was obliged to keep his word; but they could not help admiring the love and duty of Titus, who was so good a son to so unkind a father. And in that same year they chose him to be one of the chief officers of the army.

Not long after this a war broke out between the Romans and the Gauls. The Roman army, commanded by the dictator, Titus Quintius Pennus, marched out to meet the Gauls, who had encamped about three miles from Rome, near a bridge over the river Anio. Quintius pitched his camp on the other side of the river, nearer to Rome; so the bridge was between the two armies. Both tried hard to get possession of it, and there was a good deal of fighting; but neither party could keep the bridge, and at last the armies went back each to its own side of the river.

Then a gigantic Gaul came forward all alone upon the empty bridge, and waving his sword in the air, shouted aloud—

"Let the bravest man among the Romans come out and fight with me, that we may see if the Gauls or the Romans are the best warriors."

The bravest of the Roman youths stood silent for a while, ashamed to refuse to fight, yet not liking the danger of meeting so fierce an enemy. At last Titus Manlius came forward to the dictator.

"General," he said, "I should never have dared to step out of the ranks to fight without your orders,—no, not if I had been sure that I should win the victory. But, if you will give me leave, I will show this great hulking brute, who is strutting and bragging in front of the Gaulish standards, that I am come of the same race as that Manlius who threw the Gauls down the Tarpeian Rock."

"Well said, brave Manlius!" answered the dictator, "you show that your love for your country is as great as your love for your father. Go on, and by the help of the gods let these Gauls see that Rome is not to be conquered."

Then the young man's friends helped him to put on his armour. He took the shield of a foot soldier, and girt himself with a good Spanish sword. So they led him forth against the Gaul, who, as the savage custom of his people was, showed his joy at meeting his enemy by shouting out his war song, and making mocking faces at the Roman. Then the rest returned to their places, and the champions were left between the armies, who stood to watch the fight with the greatest eagerness. It was more like seeing a play acted than looking at a real combat, so different did the two warriors appear, and so unequal did they seem.

The Gaul was of gigantic size and great strength; he was clad in a garment checked with many colours, his painted armour glittered with gold, and round his neck he wore a twisted collar of gold. He carried a shield and a long and heavy broadsword. The Roman, though much smaller, was strong and active. His dress was not half so gay, and his armour was more useful than splendid. He came forward quietly, without useless shouts or wavings of his weapons, but keeping all his strength for the hard work of the battle. Thus they stood between the two armies; and the Gaul, who towered above the Roman, holding his shield before his body with his left hand, struck at Manlius with his long broadsword. So great a stroke was it that the noise of it could be heard far away as Manlius caught it on his shield, and so remained unhurt. Then, before the Gaul had time to strike again, Manlius ran close to him, and knocking up the giant's shield with his own, he plunged his short double-edged sword again and again into the body of his enemy. Down fell the Gaul, and his gigantic body lay stretched out covering a great space of ground. Manlius stooped down, and unfastening from the throat of the dead man the golden collar he wore, clasped it round his own neck, and returned to his friends. The army of the Gauls was struck with surprise and fear, but the Romans with shouts of joy and triumph led their brave young champion to the dictator. And from that day Manlius was called Torquatus, from the Latin word (torquis) which means a collar, because he had won the golden collar from the gigantic Gaul.

The end of the story of Titus Manlius is a sad one, but it is interesting. You will hear how he who gave such full obedience to his own father, and also to his general, expected the same obedience and duty from his son, and you will hear too how sternly he punished that son for the want of it.

Many years after the fight between Manlius and the Gaul there was a war between the Romans and the Latins. Manlius was then one of the consuls, and he and his fellow consul led the Roman army out and encamped before the town of Capua. The Latins were of the same race as the Romans, their manners, customs, and language were the same; and as they had been allies, many of the Romans had friends in the Latin army. The consuls, because of this, agreed together that the soldiers must be kept very strictly and severely. And they sent a crier through the camp to say that no man was to fight with the enemy out of his rank, or without the command of the consuls.

Now it happened that among the leaders of the horsemen who were sent out from the Roman camp to find out what the Latins were doing was a son of the consul Manlius, who was called Titus, as his father was. Young Manlius was very brave and full of spirit, and was eager to make his name famous by some brave deed as his father had done. One day, when he was riding out with his troop, he met a party of the enemy's horsemen, whose leader was a young man of noble family and great courage, named Geminus Mettius. Mettius knew the consul's son, and called out to him:

"What," said he, "do you Romans mean to fight the Latins with one troop of horse? What has become of your two consuls and your great army?"

"You will see what has become of them soon enough," answered Manlius. "At the battle of Lake Regillus you had as much fighting with us as you wanted; but you shall have plenty more of it before we have done with you."

Mettius laughed.

"Before that dreadful day comes," said he, "when you mean to do such wonderful things, will you dare to fight with me, that all the world may see how much braver a Latin knight is than a Roman."

Manlius was very angry at the mocking words of Mettius, and forgetting his father's commands and the decree of the consuls, he said he was ready to fight. The rest of the horsemen stood aside so as to give the two young men plenty of room for the battle, and they set spurs to their horses, and charged one another fiercely with their sharply-pointed spears. The lance of Manlius just grazed the helmet of the Latin, while Mettius slightly wounded the neck of the Roman's horse. Then turning their horses they charged again. Manlius raised himself in his saddle and pierced his enemy's horse between the ears. The horse, frightened by the pain of the wound, reared and plunged, and threw Mettius; and while he was trying to get on his feet again, Manlius ran his spear into his throat, and so killed him. Then, dismounting, he seized the arms of the Latin, carried them to his companions, and rode back in triumph with them to the Roman camp. He hastened to his father's tent, little thinking of what was going to happen.

"Father," said he, when he stood before the consul, "to show you that I am worthy to be your son, I bring you here the spoils of a Latin knight who defied and challenged me, and whom I have slain fairly in single combat."

When the consul had heard his son's words, he answered him nothing, but turned away his face. Presently he ordered the soldiers to be called together by the sound of a trumpet, and then, in the presence of all, he spoke to his son in these words:

"Titus Manlius, you have forgotten the obedience a soldier owes his general, and the respect a son should show to his father's commands, and you have dared to fight the enemy against our orders. If you were not to be punished for doing this, the Roman soldiers, who, till now, have been careful in their duty and obedient to their leaders, might grow careless, and so the army of Rome would become weak and useless. Now, therefore, I must choose whether I will do my duty to Rome and punish my son, or whether my love for my son shall make me forget my duty to Rome. I choose that you and I shall pay for our rashness and folly, but that Rome shall not be the worse.

"As for me, the love that all fathers feel for their children, and the proofs of your courage that you have just shown me, grieve me deeply; but since you must die for having disobeyed the consuls, show me that you are worthy to be my son by submitting cheerfully to the punishment."

Then he bade the lictors bind his son, which they did, and then cut off his head.

The army was greatly surprised by the severity of the consul, and very sorry for the brave young Manlius, and a splendid funeral was made for him. But the fear of being treated in the same way made the soldiers more obedient, and the guards and sentinels more watchful. This did much good in the war that followed, which ended in the victory of the Romans.

Titus Manlius Torquatus has his son beheaded

The Death of Decius
Chapter Thirteen

IN THE last story I told you how Titus Manlius loved his country better than his son. Now I am going to tell you how Publius Decius Mus, who was consul at the same time as Manlius, loved his country better than himself.

Some years before the time when Manlius and Decius were consuls together, a war broke out between the Romans and the Samnites. Valerius Corvus, who was then consul, gained a great victory over the Samnites in Campania. The other consul, Cornelius Cossus, advanced towards Samnium, and in doing so led his army through a pass in which was a narrow valley. On one side of this valley the Samnite army was hidden among the rocks, so that the Romans could not see them. The Samnites intended, as soon as all the Roman army were in the valley and trying to make their way through the narrowest part, to rush upon them and so win an easy victory. Fortunately the Romans found out that the Samnites were in ambush there before the whole army was in the valley; and while the consul was planning how he could get his soldiers safely out of this dangerous place, Publius

Decius, one of his officers, came to him. Decius had noticed that there was in the pass a hill from which all that was being done by the Samnites could be seen, and that it would be easy for lightly armed men to seize it before the enemy could prevent them.

"See you not, Cornelius," he said to the consul, "the top of yonder hill above the Samnites? If we can take that hill we shall be safe. Give me a few soldiers and let me try to take it; and if I do so, then do you march your army out of the pass without fear. For the enemy being just under the hill will not dare to follow you for fear of our attacking them behind. As to us, the good fortune of Rome and our own courage will bring us safely back to you."

The consul praised Decius for his brave plan; and having got together the soldiers he had asked for, he marched quickly and silently through the rocks, and got possession of the hill before the enemy noticed him.

The Samnites did not know what to do when they found that Decius had posted himself so well on the top of the hill. They did not dare to pursue the consul, who was now able to march the main body of the army safely out of the pass, and they were afraid to charge up the hill and attack Decius. Before they could make up their minds what to do, night came on.

Decius wondered that the Samnites did not attack him; but when evening came, he called some of his officers together and spoke to them.

"How idle or how ignorant these Samnites are," said he; "they might by this time have shut us up in ditches and walls, but not a man has begun to work. They do not seem to know what to do. But we shall be as stupid as they are if we stay here a minute longer than we need. Come on then with me; and before it grows too dark, let us see how they have placed their guards and where we may get out most easily."

Then he and some of the other officers dressed themselves like common soldiers, and so went and found out all that he wanted to know. Then he sent word to the soldiers that they should all come to him quite silently and ready armed.

"Fellow soldiers," he said, "keep silence while I speak to you, and if you agree to my plan, show me that you do so by going to my right hand. We are here surrounded by an enemy; but we are not like men who have been overtaken because they are lazy or cowardly. You won this place by your bravery, and the same bravery must help you to get out. You saved a Roman army by coming here—now save yourselves. You who delivered so many though you are so few, you need no help but your own.

We have to do with an enemy so stupid that they never found out this important hill till we had taken it. You outwitted them when they were awake; surely it will not be difficult to do so again now that they are asleep.

"There is only one way of safety left us. We must sally out and make our way through the Samnites who surround us. Now they are all sound asleep, and you shall try to pass through them in silence without their knowing that you are there; but if they wake, then astonish them by setting up a sudden outcry and dreadful shouts, and cut your way through them with your good swords. And now, let those of you who think my plan a good one pass to my right hand."

Every man of them went to his right hand, and Decius at once led them down the hill, and into the enemy's camp.

They had got safely to the middle of the camp, when one of the Romans as he stepped across the guards who were lying fast asleep, happened to stumble against a shield, which gave such a clang that the sentinel to whom it belonged awoke. Starting up he woke the man next him, who gave the alarm to others. At first the Samnites did not know whether these strangers were friends or enemies, whether they were the Romans on the hill, or whether they were some of the consul's soldiers come back to attack them. But Decius now commanded his men to set up a shout, which they did, and so startled and amazed the Samnites that they were all confused and did not know what to do. So Decius and his soldiers, striking down the guards who tried to stop them, broke through, and got safely away from their foes.

It was still dark, and when they had got quite out of danger, Decius stopped and spoke to his followers.

"This noble deed of yours, my brave Romans," he said, "will be praised and admired for many a hundred years. But now, you deserve better than that darkness and silence should cover you when you return with so much glory to the camp. Here, therefore, let us rest and wait for day."

The soldiers obeyed him gladly, and as soon as it was light he sent a messenger to the consul to tell him of their coming. As soon as the soldiers in the Roman camp heard that the brave men who had risked their lives to save the army were coming back safe, they ran out to meet them with thanks and praises, calling them deliverers, and giving thanks to the gods. When Decius and his followers came to the consul's tent, Cornelius called all the army together by sound of trumpet, and began to make a speech to them in praise of Decius.

But Decius interrupted him.

"General," he said, "do not waste the time in praising me, but take the chance and attack the Samnites while they are still in fear and wonder."

The consul took his advice, and the army at once marched back and charged the enemy, who did not expect them, and were quite unprepared.

Many of the Samnites were unarmed and straggling about the pass. The Romans easily drove them back into their camp, and then followed them there, took and plundered it, and killed a great many of the Samnites.

Next day the consul called the Roman army together, and finished making the speech in praise of Decius, which had been interrupted the day before. Many rich presents were given to Decius, and among them was a crown of gold. His brave soldiers too were well rewarded.

I must now go on to that war against the Latins, in which young Titus Manlius was put to death by his father's order. The elder Manlius and Decius were consuls at that time, as I told you. After the death of the young man, the two consuls resolved to fight a battle with the Latins, and they drew up their army in proper order, Manlius leading the right and Decius the left wing. At first they fought on both sides with the same bravery, but after a while the Romans on the left wing, who were commanded by Decius, found the Latins too strong for them, and began to give way.

When Decius saw this he called to him Marcus Valerius, the high priest of the Romans, and said,

"I see, Valerius, that we are now in want of the help of the gods. Do you now, therefore, say the solemn words with which I may devote myself for our army, and I will repeat them after you."

The Romans believed that a general could certainly win victory for his army by devoting himself as they called it. The general must say some very solemn words, standing in one particular way, and wearing a certain dress. Then if he let himself be killed directly afterwards, they believed that the army against which he was fighting would certainly be destroyed.

Valerius told Decius to put on a long embroidered purple mantle, and to cover his head with it; then to stand with both his feet on a spear, while he said after him these words:—

"O Jupiter, Mars, and all ye heavenly and infernal gods, I ask your pardon and I pray for your favour. I pray that you will give victory and power to the people of Rome, and strike their enemies with fear and death. And for the good of the people of Rome, I here devote the army of the enemy and myself to the infernal gods."

When he had said this prayer, he sent a messenger to

the other consul, Manlius, to tell him what he had done. Then, girding his purple mantle round him and taking his arms, he mounted his horse and spurred into the midst of the enemy. To both armies he seemed wonderful, more like a god than a man. Wherever he came he terrified the Latins; he rode right through their front ranks, and then charged into their main body, while they stood trembling, struck with fear and awe. And when at last he fell, beaten down by numbers, the Latins began to give back in their terror, while the Romans fell upon them with redoubled courage.

When Manlius heard of what Decius had done, he wept for him and praised him for daring to die for Rome.

Decius charges into the Latins, sacrificing himself for Rome

Then he led on some of the Roman troops who had not yet fought.

"Forward!" he said. "Remember your country and your parents, your wives and children, and more than all remember your noble consul, who gave himself to die that you might win the victory."

The soldiers, full of hope and courage, charged the Latins with such fury that they defeated them, killed a great number, and put the rest to flight.

The body of the brave Decius could not be found that day, for it was late when the battle was over, and evening was coming on. But next morning it was found lying covered with darts and spears among a heap of Latins whom he had killed. Manlius made a splendid funeral for him, as his great courage well deserved.

The Caudine Forks
Chapter Fourteen

SOME DISTANCE to the south of Rome, among the Apennine mountains, lay the country of Samnium, where lived a brave and warlike people, who were for many years at war with the Romans.

The general of the Samnites, at the time I am going to tell you about, was called Caius Pontius. He was a brave and skillful soldier, the son of a very wise old man, whose name was Herennius.

When Pontius heard that the Romans were marching against Samnium, he led his army to a place called Caudium, in the mountains between Rome and his own country. He made some of his soldiers take off their armour and dress themselves like shepherds. Then he sent them towards the Roman camp, driving sheep before them—so that the Roman sentinels, when they saw them, thought they were real shepherds. The Romans took the disguised Samnite soldiers prisoners, and led them before their consul, Spurius Postumius.

Postumius asked the Samnites, whom he supposed to be shepherds, to tell him anything they could about the

Samnite army—where it was, and what it was doing. They answered him, as their general had told them to do, that the Samnite army was gone into Apulia in the south of Italy, and that it was besieging Luceria, a town whose people were friends and allies of the Romans. Now, as these pretended shepherds all told the same story, Postumius thought it must be true, and he determined to go to the help of the Lucerians.

The shortest road to Luceria was past Caudium, where, as I told you, Pontius and his army really were. Near Caudium is a place called the Caudine Forks—and I will try to describe it to you, that you may understand what afterwards happened. The road to Caudium went through a very narrow pass or valley between two steep rocky cliffs; on the other side of the pass, the valley widened out into a large green meadow or plain covered with grass, and quite surrounded by steep hills.

The road went across this plain and then through another little pass between rocks steeper and more difficult even than the first. These two passes were called the Caudine Forks.

The Roman army marched through the first pass, and across the plain without any difficulty, but when they got to the second pass their surprise was great to find the road blocked up with piles of great stones, and with trees which had been cut down and thrown across it, so that neither man nor horse could get through. At the same time they saw the Samnite army appear on the hills above the pass, so as to prevent them from going round.

As quickly as they could, the Romans turned and retreated across the plain to the pass by which they had come; but when they got there they found that the way out was blocked in the same manner, and guarded too by Samnite troops. All along the tops of the hills round them they could see their enemies, whom Pontius had placed there, and they felt that they were shut in hopelessly, and were so astonished that they stood for a long time as still as statues, not knowing which way to turn, or what to do. At last they set to work to pitch their camp and to fortify it, though they saw very well how useless the work was, and knew that the Samnites might, if they pleased, keep them shut up in that deep valley, till they were starved to death. The Samnite soldiers looked on, and laughed and mocked at the unhappy Romans, who turned to their generals and asked from them the comfort and help which the generals could not give.

By and by the night came on, and the soldiers gathering together, began to talk over their dreadful position, and to make plans as to what was to be done.

"Let us break through the blockade," said one, "and force our way along the road."

"Were it not better," cried another, "to climb up the mountain sides and through the woods,—any way so that we carry our swords with us and that we may come at the enemy? If we could only get at them, it would be easy enough to us Romans to fight these pitiful Samnites, whom we have beaten so often in the last thirty years.

"Pooh!" said a third. "How can we possibly get at the enemy, with these steep hills hanging almost over our heads. What does it matter whether we are armed or unarmed, whether we are brave men or cowards? We are caught like rats in a trap, and the Samnites need not even trouble themselves to draw their swords to kill us, but may sit still and watch us die."

In such talk they passed the night, caring neither to take food or sleep.

The Samnites did not know what to do, or what would be the best way to use their victory. At last they decided to send to Herennius Pontius, the father of their general, who, as I said, was a very wise man, and ask him what they had better do. Herennius was now very old, and was living a quiet life away from the toils both of war and of government But though his body was so weak, his mind was strong, and his advice was very much respected by all the Samnite people.

When his son's messengers came to him, he sent back word that the Samnites had better let the Roman army go home safe and unhurt. The Samnites did not like this message at all, and told the messengers to go a second time to Herennius, and ask him again what they should do.

"Let them kill every one of the Romans," said Herennius.

When these words were told to the Samnites, they began to think that the old man's mind must be growing as weak as his body, and that he could have no meaning in sending two such different messages. Still, they thought Herennius so wise, that they sent the messengers a third time, to persuade him to come to their camp, that they might hear what he really thought with their own ears. So the old man was laid in a cart, and driven to the Samnite camp; and when he got there he spoke to them in these words:—

"I advised you to let the Romans go safely home, because if you do so great a kindness to this brave people, you will make them your firm friends for ever. But if you will not do this you must kill them all, so that they may not return to fight you again; for the shame of their defeat will make them hate you more than ever, and they will be more fierce and dreadful enemies than they are now. If you will not do either of these things I have no third advice to give you."

Then Pontius asked him if it would not be better to spare the lives of the Romans, but to make them promise that they would not fight against the Samnites again.

"By doing this," answered Herennius, "you will neither make the Romans your friends nor prevent them from being your enemies. They are such a proud and brave people that if you disgrace them they will never forgive you, and will never rest till they have punished you and revenged themselves."

But Pontius and his army would not take the old man's advice, so he went home again.

By this time the Romans began to be in great want of food. They had made several attempts to get out of the valley, but they were always beaten back. At last the consuls sent messengers to Pontius, to try and make peace, or, if he would not make peace, to challenge him to battle. Pontius sent back word that the battle was already won; that the Romans were his prisoners, and must lay down their arms, and all pass under the yoke; and that the consuls must promise that Rome would be at peace with Samnium.

The yoke was made by planting two spears upright in the ground, and tying a third spear to their tops, so as to make a sort of arch through which the army had to pass. It was the custom at this time in Italy to make a beaten army pass under the yoke, and this was considered a great disgrace, because it showed that the army was completely conquered.

The consuls knew that they had no power to promise that Rome would keep peace with Samnium; but they thought that if they did not promise, the Samnites would kill all their army, and they wished to save their men, so they agreed to do all that Pontius wished.

When the Roman soldiers heard that the Samnite general had sent word that they must all pass under the yoke, there was as much grief and sorrow in the camp as if he had said they should all be put to the sword. They cried out against the consuls who had led them into such danger and disgrace. They thought how shameful it would be to give up their armour and weapons. They fancied how their proud enemies would insult and mock at them, and how sad would be their return to Rome, whence they had started with such joyful hopes of victory.

"We," cried they, "are the only army in the world that ever was beaten without a battle—without a sword being drawn—who wore arms only to give them up to our mortal enemies without striking a blow; and whose strength and courage were good for nothing but to make us feel our disgrace more bitterly."

While they bemoaned themselves in this way, the word of command was given that they should march out of the camp, each man wearing only one garment, and leaving his armour and weapons behind him. First, the consuls, having taken off their splendid robes and rich armour, were obliged to march under the yoke, then came the nobles and officers, and lastly the soldiers. The Samnites stood round jeering and laughing at the unfortunate Romans, who would almost rather have been killed, than have had to bear such disgrace. When they had marched out of the Caudine Pass, and had got away from the Samnites, they might easily have reached Capua, a town which was friendly to Rome, before night came on; but they were so miserable, and so dreadfully ashamed of being seen in such a condition, that they chose to stay away from the town, meaning to sleep on the bare ground, though they had neither food nor clothing, nor tents to shelter them.

But news was brought to the people of Capua that the Roman army was just outside the town in this sad state. The Capuans were very sorry to hear it, and immediately they sent out plenty of clothes and food for the soldiers, and to the consuls they sent arms and horses, and splendid garments such as suited their high rank. When the Romans had eaten and clothed themselves, they marched into Capua. The people came out to meet them with their nobles at their head, and welcomed their visitors with kind words; they took them into their houses, and treated them like dear friends. But the Romans were so unhappy that all the kindness of the Capuans could hardly get them to speak a word, or even to lift up their eyes from the ground. The next day they went away to Rome, seeming more ashamed and miserable than ever, and not speaking a word as they marched along.

Now, by this time, news of the great misfortune at Caudium had got to Rome, and the whole city was full of mourning and grief. The shops were shut up, the courts of law were closed, the nobles left off the splendid scarlet and purple edged robes they generally wore, the ladies put away their golden ornaments, and all the people showed in every way how great was their sorrow, for the disgrace that had fallen on the name of Rome. At first the people were very angry with the soldiers, and said that they ought not to be allowed to come into the city at all. But when the army arrived, their anger changed to pity;

for the unhappy men came marching into the town at night, that they might not be seen, and each soldier went at once silently to his own house, and shut himself up there—so that for days after not one of them was to be seen out of doors in the streets. The consuls, too, shut themselves up in the same way, and all they would do was to name a dictator who should govern the city till other consuls could be chosen. As soon as could be, the new consuls called Postumius before them, that he might tell them about the shameful peace that he had made with the Samnites at Caudium.

Postumius came into their presence, with looks as sad and unhappy as on the day when he had to pass under the yoke.

"I know well enough," said he, "that you have called me here not for honour but for shame, and that I am commanded to speak as one who is guilty of a badly managed war and a shameful peace. I will only say to defend myself that I agreed to that peace to save your army from being destroyed. But I think that as it was made without the people of Rome knowing anything about it, they need not keep the promises that I made. Instead of keeping the agreement, give up to the Samnites the men who made these promises. Were you Romans ever asked if you would agree to the peace?

Who can pretend that you have deceived them? You never promised anything to the Samnites, and you never ordered us to make any agreements for you. We are the men who promised, and as we cannot keep our word, we will give our lives instead. Give us up to the Samnites then, and let them do what they please with us, and in the meantime let the consuls raise and arm all the soldiers they can, and begin the war over again with better success."

The senate and consuls were very sorry for the brave Postumius, but they and all the people could find no better way of freeing themselves from the treaty of peace to which he had been forced to agree. Every one praised him for being ready to give his life for his country, and the Romans were so filled with anger and so eager for war, that a great army was soon raised, and, with the consuls at its head, marched towards Caudium.

Before the army went the heralds with Postumius and the others who were to be given up to the Samnites. When they came near to the gate of Caudium, the heralds told the soldiers to bind the hands of these men behind their backs, which was done. The soldier who tied the hands of Postumius felt such sorrow and respect for his old general, that he fastened the cords very gently and loosely.

"Draw the cord tighter," said Postumius, "that the law may be obeyed, as is just and right."

Then the heralds led him and the others before Pontius and the Samnite nobles, and said to them,

"These persons, without the leave of the Roman people, have promised to make peace with you. The Roman people will have no peace with the Samnites, and they send you these men to do with them what you will."

Pontius and all the Samnites were extremely angry at this, for they thought that the Roman people ought to have kept the promises that their consul had made. And after a while Pontius said,

"Neither I nor the Samnites will accept these men, whom you pretend to give up to us. I do not blame you, Postumius, who, like a brave and honourable man, have come to give up your life as you cannot keep your promise. But if the Roman people do not like the agreement their consul made for them, let them bring their army back again into the place where we surrounded them. Let them take their arms again, and shut themselves up in their camp and let all be as it was before the consuls made the treaty. Is this your truth? Is this how you keep your word? You have your soldiers safe as I promised you; but where is the peace that you promised to me? I will not accept these men whom you pretend to deliver up to me;

but I call upon the gods to punish you for breaking your solemn vows. Go, lictor, unbind these Romans, and let them go wherever they please."

This was soon done, and Postumius and the other prisoners went back unharmed to the Roman camp.

The Samnites now began to understand how wise had been the advice of old Herennius, when he told them either to make friends of the Romans by setting them free, or to kill them all. For the war that began again was fiercer and more cruel than ever.

The Two Fabii
Chapter Fifteen

THE SAMNITES had lost many battles in the wars with Rome, and the Romans began to hope that soon they might be able quite to conquer this brave people, who had fought for so many years against them. Quintus Fabius was now consul; he was the son of Fabius Maximus, a brave old man who had been many times consul, and had won many victories for Rome. Quintus Fabius was young and brave, and thought that, as the Samnites had been so often beaten, it would be easy for him to beat them again, and he hoped that he might have the joy and glory of at last finishing the war. So he raised an army, and marched to attack them.

The Samnites, however, were a very brave people, and they did not much fear Fabius, knowing that he was young and had not had much practice as a general. They, too, got an army together, and set out towards Rome.

I said that Quintus Fabius was a brave man, like the rest of his family, who have been called "the brave Fabian race." But he forgot that he ought to be watchful and careful as well as brave. As he marched through

Campania, he came in sight of a party of soldiers sent out by the Samnite general in front of his army, to see if the way was clear for the rest. When this small body of troops saw the Romans coming towards them they retreated to their fellow countrymen. Fabius thought they were running away from him, and at once ordered his soldiers to follow them as fast as possible. Meantime the Samnite general, hearing that the Romans were coming, had placed his soldiers in order of battle, and was ready for the attack. The Romans came up, tired before the battle began, because they had marched so fast; their ranks were in disorder, and they looked as if they were coming to plunder and not to fight. It is not hard to guess what happened. The Samnites easily resisted the charge of the Romans, drove them back, killed three thousand of them, and wounded many more; and if it had not grown too dark for the battle to go on, the whole army would have been destroyed.

Fabius did his best to get his men together again, and made them dig ditches and make mounds round their camp to defend themselves as well as they could in the darkness and hurry. But they had lost all their baggage in the flight, and here there was no food for the hungry, no comforts for the wounded, hardly even rest for the tired; for they feared that the conquering Samnites would follow and attack them again. They waited for the coming of the daylight in this miserable state, thinking that surely that night would be their last.

"For how," they said, "can men tired with want of sleep, weak with their wounds, and out of heart with the shame of being beaten—how can such men do battle against an enemy who conquered us when we were full of hope and courage?"

Fortunately it happened that the Samnite general heard that the other consul was marching against him with another army. This was not true, but the Samnite believed it, and thinking it best to be contented with the victory he had already won, he led his army away, and so Fabius and his troops were saved.

The people of Rome were very angry when they heard that Fabius had been defeated, and they thought the disgrace was worse even than the loss of men. They had hoped that the war was nearly at an end, and now because of the consul's rashness and carelessness things were as bad as ever. The Senate commanded that the consul should come to Rome to answer for what he had done. But when he came before them the rage of the people was so great that they would hardly let him speak to defend himself. They felt that he ought to have been wiser, since he was the son of so brave and successful a general, and that he had disgraced the name of Rome and the name of Fabius by his rashness.

The elder Fabius feared that his son would be disgraced and turned out of his place as consul, and he came forward before the Senate to defend him.

"I cannot excuse his fault," said the old man; "but I pray you that you will not so shame me who have done some service to Rome, and yet more that you will not disgrace the family of Fabius which, almost from the building of Rome till now, has given so many brave men to serve their country.

"And yet I would not have you pardon my son because of the great deeds of his ancestors; but I feel sure that he will yet do good work for Rome, because he has learned to love his country better than even his family. You have seen the worst that can happen from his rashness—but the good is yet to come which you may expect from a man of so brave a temper, and who has been bred up by myself, a master, as you know, able to teach him what a warrior should be. Many men have learned by misfortunes to be more careful, and so may he. If you will let him try again, what has been done wrong shall be amended. I will answer for my son to the people. I will go with him to battle as his lieutenant, and share his fortune whatever it may be. I am old, but I have courage enough and strength enough still to bear the toils of war. If I were good for nothing else, yet I could cheer our own men and terrify the enemy by reminding them of my old battles; and besides I can advise and direct the young consul. Did I not know my son's temper and feel sure that he will be ready to follow good advice, I should be sorry to risk the fame I have won in so many years of toil and danger just now when my life is near its end."

The people felt that what Fabius Maximus said was quite true, and they agreed to what he asked. Everything was soon got ready to begin the war again, and the consul and his father led the army away from Rome. The consul was willing to do all that his father advised, and the soldiers were eager to show that they could do better than in their last fight. They trusted too in the brave old Fabius, remembering how often their fathers led by him had beaten the Samnites; and they wished with all their hearts for battle.

The armies met, the fight began, and at first the Romans got the worst of it. The Samnite general, with a number of his bravest troops, surrounded the consul; but when Fabius Maximus saw his son's danger, he rode at full speed into the midst of the Samnites to rescue him. The Roman horse soldiers saw him, and feeling how shameful it would be if such an old man should dare to do more than they who were both young and strong, they followed him, and charged the enemy so fiercely that the consul was saved and the battle won. The Samnite general, who was a brave man and a good soldier, did his best to keep his men firm and to stop those who fled. But in trying to do so he lost the chance of escaping himself, and was taken prisoner by the Romans, with a great many of his soldiers, and many more were slain. The Samnite camp was also taken, and a great deal of rich plunder, and the two Fabii went home in triumph.

The two Fabii in battle with the Samnites

How King Pyrrhus Fought Against Rome
Chapter Sixteen

As years went on the power of the Romans grew greater. They conquered many of the towns round Rome, and made the people their subjects and allies. So year after year their armies went further away from Rome, and sometimes had to go quite to the southern part of Italy.

On the seacoasts of southern Italy were many towns which had been built by Greeks, who had sailed over the sea from Greece, and made new homes for themselves in Italy.

There was a quarrel between the people of one of these towns, which was called Tarentum, and the Romans. The Tarentines attacked some Roman ships; and the Roman senate, hearing of this, sent Lucius Postumius as ambassador to complain of the wrong that had been done. When he arrived at Tarentum, he was received with the greatest rudeness by the people. He tried to make a speech to them, but they laughed at his way of speaking

Greek, and at his dress, which was a long white cloak or toga, edged with scarlet, in the Roman fashion. They mocked at Postumius and would not listen to him, and at last a rude fellow threw dirt at him. Postumius held up his white cloak stained with dirt to show the people, who only laughed the more.

"Laugh on, Tarentines, while you can," cried the Roman; "soon enough ye shall weep instead; for I tell you that this gown shall be washed white in your blood."

Having said this he left Tarentum and went back to Rome.

The senate and people were very angry that their ambassador should have been so insulted, and at once declared war against Tarentum.

The Tarentines soon found that they were not strong enough to fight against the Romans alone, and they resolved to ask help from Greece.

Now there lived at this time in a country called Epirus, which was part of Greece, a great and warlike king, whose name was Pyrrhus. He was a good general, and he wished to win for himself a great name in war. He had a splendid army, and the Greek soldiers were then thought to be the best in the world. They fought in heavy armour, armed with long spears, and standing close together shoulder to shoulder; while the Romans, as you know, used short swords, and fought in looser order, that is, not quite so close to one another. The Greeks also used elephants in war, and these animals had at this time never been seen in Italy.

The Tarentines resolved that they would send and invite King Pyrrhus to come over and help them.

"These barbarian Romans," they said, "will never be able to resist so brave and skillful a king, with his splendid troops and his terrible elephants."

Pyrrhus was pleased with the plan, and agreed to cross over to Italy to help the Tarentines. He made great preparations for war, and got together a large number of ships, some of which were vessels of war and some were transports, ships, that is, for carrying his soldiers and their horses across the sea.

News was brought to Rome that the King of Epirus was going to invade Italy with a great army. The Romans knew that they must do their best against such an enemy. They got together several large armies, and even the poorest people were obliged to go for soldiers, which they had never had to do before. Troops and money were collected from their allies, and everything was made ready for a great war. Meantime Pyrrhus and his army arrived in Italy, after a very stormy voyage, in which some of his ships were wrecked. He went to Tarentum, and he had not been there long before the Tarentines began to be very sorry that they had ever invited him to come. For they found that they had got a master instead of an ally. Pyrrhus governed the city as if it had belonged to him. He shut up their theatres and places of amusement: he made all the young men soldiers, and punished them very severely if they did not attend properly to their drill. Many of them tried to leave the town, but Pyrrhus shut the gates and guarded them with his Greek soldiers, and so kept the Tarentines at home whether they liked it or not.

When the Roman armies were ready, the Consul Valerius Lævinus led them against Pyrrhus. The king heard that they were coming, and he wrote this letter to the consul,—

"I hear that you are coming against the Tarentines with an army. Leave your army, and come to me with only a few men. Let me know what your quarrel with the Tarentines is about, and I will force one side to do to the other what is just."

To this letter the consul sent the following answer,—

"We will not make you our judge, nor do we fear you as an enemy. We think you are impertinent to meddle with the doings of other men, and to dare to come to Italy without our leave. And we have come with our armies to fight you as well as the Tarentines."

Then Lævinus led his army on, and pitched his camp on the bank of the river Siris. Soon afterwards he crossed the river, and the two armies met in the plain, on the farther side from the Roman camp, near a town called Heraclea.

King Pyrrhus was a brave soldier as well as a skillful general, and he charged the Romans at the head of his troops. The Romans could easily see which was the king by his splendid armour, and by the bravery with which he led on his soldiers and cheered them to the fight. They tried hard to reach Pyrrhus, and he was in great danger, so that at last he gave his glittering arms and scarlet mantle to Megacles, one of his officers. He knew that if he were killed the Romans would win the victory, for the Greeks would not dare to fight without their brave king.

The battle was long and fierce; the Romans were eager to win the glory of killing King Pyrrhus, and at last Megacles was slain. When the Greeks saw the horseman in the well-known armour of the king struck down, they thought Pyrrhus was killed, and were so terrified that they began to retreat. But Pyrrhus threw off his helmet, and rode bare-headed through the ranks that all men might see him; calling to the soldiers at the same time in a loud voice, bidding them look at him and see that he was alive and with them.

In this way he so much cheered his soldiers that they attacked the Romans with redoubled fury. The Consul

Lævinus, seeing that his men were disheartened, ordered his horse soldiers, whom he had kept out of the battle till now, to charge, hoping that these fresh troops would drive the Epirotes before them. But Pyrrhus had not yet brought his elephants into the fight, and now when the Roman horse charged, he commanded that the elephants should advance.

The Romans had never seen these monstrous creatures before, and they and their horses were so much terrified that they turned and fled. By running among the rest of the Roman army, they put it into confusion, and in spite of all that Lævinus could do, they were forced to retreat across the river, and lost their camp and many men.

A great number of the Greeks too were killed, and when Pyrrhus found how many of his soldiers had died he said,

"If I gain another victory such as this, I shall have to go home without a man left me."

He went the next day to look at the field of battle, and when he saw the Romans lying dead, with their faces turned to the enemy (which showed that they had died fighting, and had not been killed in running away), he cried out,

"Oh, how easy would it be for me to conquer the world, if I had the Romans for my soldiers!"

He admired the courage of the Romans so much, that he tried to persuade those who were taken prisoners to join his army; and though none of them would fight against Rome, he treated them with great kindness.

After this victory Pyrrhus marched up to the north, and at last got to a town only twenty miles from Rome. Here he heard that Lævinus had got another army together, and was following him from the south of Italy, while the other consul who had been fighting the Etruscans had now made peace with them, and was marching to attack Pyrrhus from the north.

So the king gave up the hope of getting to Rome, and went back again to the south of Italy. The Roman Senate now sent ambassadors to Pyrrhus, to persuade him to take ransom for the Romans who had been taken prisoners. Among these ambassadors was Caius Fabricius, a very noble Roman, who was well known as a brave soldier and a good man.

When the ambassadors came to the king, Pyrrhus said to them,—

"I like not what you propose to me. You would have me give you up my prisoners, and if I do so, you will use them to fight against me again; and you offer me money in exchange. Now, I am not so poor as to want money from the Romans. I would rather be friends with them and give them money. Make peace with me, and you shall have my prisoners back without ransom, and I will give you rich presents besides."

Then the king said he wished to talk alone with Fabricius, and when they were by themselves he spoke to him thus:

"I wish to have all the Romans for my friends, but you, Fabricius, more than any of the others; for I have heard how noble and brave you are. I hear, however, that you are very poor. This must not be, and I will give you so much gold that you shall be richer than any other Roman. For I think it is fitting for a prince to enrich great men who are poor, and who love honour more than money. I only ask in return that you should persuade the Roman senate to make peace with me. And, when this is done, if you will go home with me to Epirus I will make you my dearest friend and the greatest man next to myself in Greece."

Then Fabricius answered the king:

"If I am said to be skillful in war or in other things, I need say no more about it, or about my being poor, as you have heard these things from other men. It is true that I have only a small cottage and a piece of land, where I live by working with my own hands. Yet, if you think that, because I am poor, I am worse off than any other Roman, you are greatly mistaken. I am a leader of my people in war. I am chosen by them to rule them, or to go as their ambassador. What does it matter to me that I am poor, while I do my duty to my country in such ways as these?

"When I compare myself with rich men, I think myself happy. My piece of land gives me all that I want. My hard work makes me sleep well, and care little what sort of food I eat; if my clothes are warm, I do not want them to be fine. So, poor as I am, I think myself richer than you. For though you were master of Epirus, you could not be satisfied without taking Italy too.

"I have been consul, and have led the Roman armies against the Lucanians and other peoples. I took their rich towns and won great spoils from them; and after paying the soldiers and all the cost of the war, I put the rest of the money into the public treasury. Since I would not make myself rich when I might have done so rightly and honourably, do you think I will now take bribes and presents from a foreign enemy?"

Pyrrhus went on to make Fabricius still larger offers, but the Roman only answered:

"If you think me an honest man, why do you try to bribe me? If you think me dishonest, why do you want to gain me?"

So Fabricius went away. But two days afterwards

Pyrrhus sent for him again. While they were talking, Pyrrhus gave a signal; a curtain was drawn back, and Fabricius saw a great elephant which had been put behind it by the king's order. The elephant lifted its trunk up over the Roman's head, and roared fiercely; but Fabricius only turned to Pyrrhus, and said with a smile:

"Your gold could not buy me yesterday, and your elephant cannot frighten me today."

Pyrrhus was much pleased with the courage of Fabricius, and he allowed the Romans, whom he had taken prisoners, to go back to Rome to pay visits to their families. For the king trusted to the word of Fabricius,

King Pyrrhus talks with Fabricius

who promised that all these prisoners would come back to him when they had seen their friends in Rome. And so honest and truthful were the Romans in those times, that every man of them came back on the day that had been fixed.

Still the Senate would make no peace with Pyrrhus while he stayed in Italy; and the next year another great battle was fought at a place called Asculum, in which the Romans were again beaten. But they fought so fiercely that Pyrrhus said when the battle was over:—

"If I have to conquer the Romans again in such a battle as this, I shall be quite undone."

There was no more fighting that year; but next year Fabricius was chosen consul, and he and his fellow consul, Quintus Æmilius, took the command of the Roman army. Pyrrhus, hearing this, led out his army against them, and encamped not far from the place where the consuls had pitched their camp.

One day a Greek slave belonging to Pyrrhus came to Fabricius, and asked to see him alone.

"I come to make you an offer," he said. "If the Roman senate will pay me well, I will give poison to King Pyrrhus in his wine cup, and so he shall die and trouble Rome no more."

Fabricius was shocked at the wickedness of the slave,

and he wrote a letter to Pyrrhus telling him of the plot.

"You seem," wrote Fabricius, "to judge very ill both of your friends and enemies, for you make war on good and true men, and trust traitors and villains. We send you word of this plot, lest your death should bring disgrace on us—lest it should be thought that we wanted to end the war by letting you be killed, if we could not end it by our valour."

When Pyrrhus read this letter, he cried out—

"Noble Fabricius! It would be easier to turn the sun out of his course than to make Fabricius do a wrong thing."

After these things Pyrrhus left Italy and made war in Sicily, where he stayed for three years. He then came back to Italy, meaning to try once more to conquer Rome.

Manlius Curius Dentatus was chosen consul when the news reached Rome that Pyrrhus was marching again to attack them. He at once began to collect an army; but the people were afraid to go as soldiers when they heard that the terrible king of Epirus was coming against them once more. Curius saw their fear, and when the first man refused to answer to his name, the consul ordered that he should be sold for a slave; "for," said he, "Rome does not want a son who is not obedient."

His commands were obeyed, and the people were now

eager to join the army, fearing lest he should treat them in the same way. So the legions were soon filled up, and the consul marched to meet the enemy.

Curius placed his army on some hills near the town of Beneventum, and Pyrrhus marched into the plain at the foot of the hills in the night. When morning came, the Romans were surprised to see the Greeks so near. Curius at once led his soldiers out of their camp and charged the foremost of the Greeks, put them to flight, and took several of their elephants. Delighted with this success, he led the Romans down into the plain, and attacked the main body of the king's army.

The army of Pyrrhus was very different now from what it had been when he first came to Italy. Most of his brave Epirot soldiers who had fought with him in many battles both in Greece and Italy had been killed, and instead of them he had filled his ranks with new men.

The Romans fought bravely, and after a while the Greeks began to give way. Pyrrhus saw this and brought up his elephants, but the Romans no longer feared them. They had found out that these animals are afraid of fire, and they had got ready bundles of sticks dipped in pitch, which they lighted and threw onto the backs of the elephants or into the little towers in which the people sat who rode on the creatures.

The elephants, being frightened by the burning sticks, and hurt by the wounds the Romans gave them with their swords and spears, turned round and ran among the Greeks, trampling down and killing a great many of them, and putting the rest into great confusion.

So ended the battle. Great numbers of the Greeks were killed, many were taken prisoners, and the rest, with Pyrrhus himself, fled to Tarentum. The king at once left Italy and sailed away to Greece, where he was killed not long afterwards.

The Senate ordered that Curius should enter the city in triumph, and never had there been so glorious a sight in Rome as was seen that day. The houses were gaily decked with wreaths of flowers and green boughs; every window was filled with eager faces, and the streets were thronged with joyful crowds, all watching to see the great procession pass by. We may fancy how glad were the hearts of the Roman people when they thought that the terrible Greeks were conquered, and how grateful they felt to the brave soldiers who had borne hardship and danger, and risked death for the sake of Rome.

First in the procession walked the senators who had gone to the gates of the city to meet the victors. Then, guarded by Roman soldiers, came the spoils taken from the enemy, piled on high wagons or carried by men.

Beautiful pictures and statues, splendid robes and stuffs of bright colours, armour adorned with gold and jewels, all sorts of beautiful things which were used and made by the skillful Greeks, but such as had never been seen before by the rougher, simpler people of Rome, were there. There too were seen for the first time in Rome those strange and terrible elephants, of which they had heard so much in the war. What surprise must the people have felt at the great creatures, their vast size, their strange snake-like trunks, the castles on their backs, in which several soldiers could sit, and the gentleness which made it possible to lead them through the crowded streets.

Then came the long line of prisoners, some of them soldiers from the towns of southern Italy, such as had often, no doubt, been seen in Rome before. But besides these there were the Greeks of Pyrrhus, his foot soldiers, the finest in the world, and his gallant horse soldiers, whose looks and dress and arms were all strange to the eyes of the people of Rome. When these had passed, the general's lictors marched by one after another, their fasces, or bundles of rods and axes, wreathed with laurel boughs. Then came the triumphal car, drawn by four beautiful horses, in which was Curius himself. He wore a splendid mantle or toga embroidered with gold, and was crowned with a laurel wreath, and in his right hand he carried a laurel bough. Behind him rode his chief officers, and the rest of the army followed, with laurel garlands twisted round their spears, singing and shouting the praises of their leader.

The procession moved slowly through the crowded streets and up to the Capitol, where Curius laid his laurel wreath at the feet of the statue of Jove, and thanked the god for the victory that he had given to Rome.